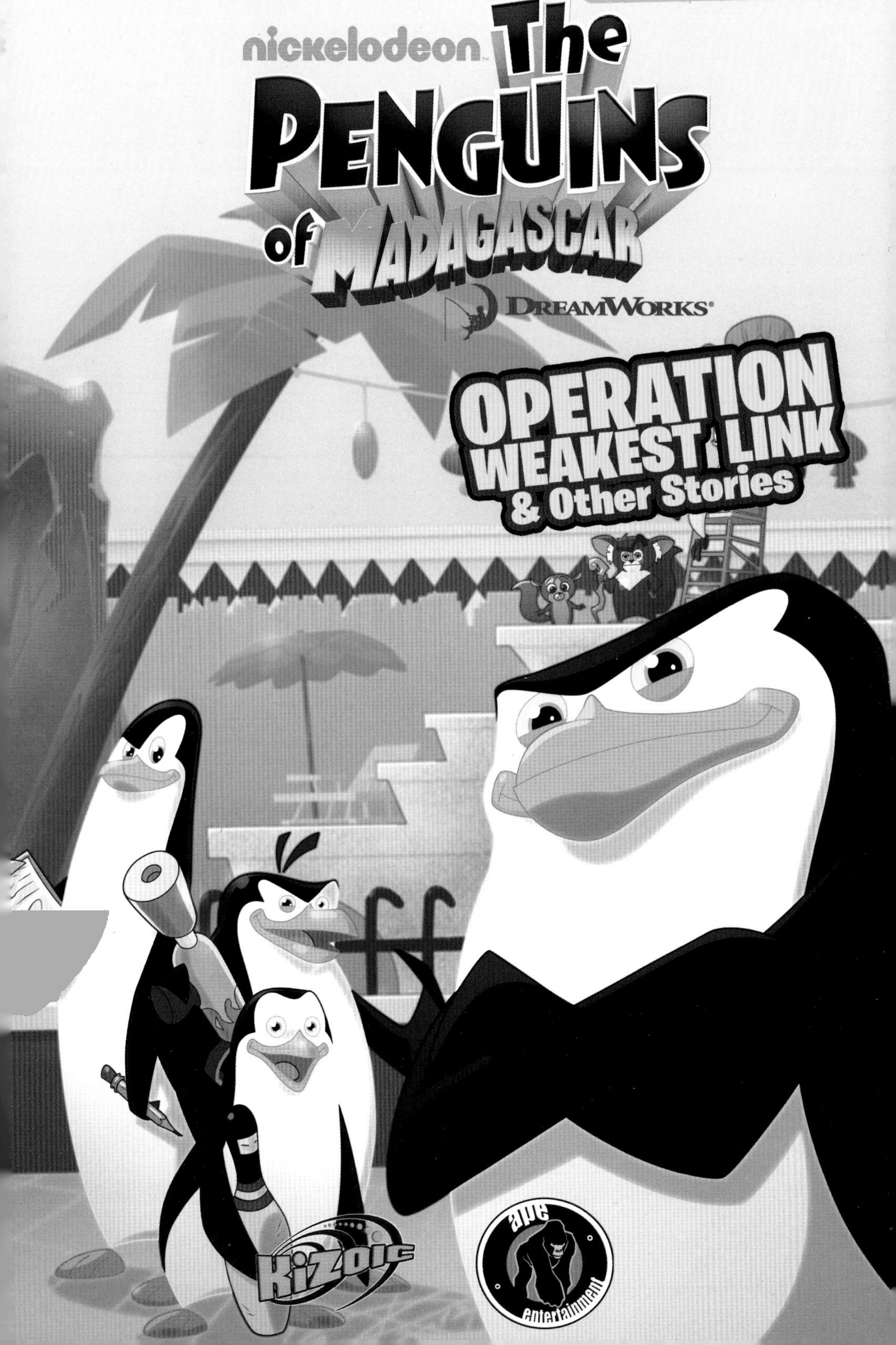
nickelodeon
The PENGUINS of MADAGASCAR
DREAMWORKS
OPERATION WEAKEST LINK
& Other Stories
KiZOIC
ape entertainment

APE ENTERTAINMENT

David Hedgecock
CEO | Partner
DHedgecock@Ape-Entertainment.com

Brent E. Erwin
COO | Partner
BErwin@Ape-Entertainment.com

Weldon Adams
Editor
WAdams@Ape-Entertainment.com

Aaron Sparrow
Editor
ASparrow@Ape-Entertainment.com

Isaiah Samson
Assistant Editor
ISamson@Ape-Entertainment.com

Rolando Mallada
Lead Artist on Staff

Marcello Ferreira
Artist on Staff

Aurelio Mazzara
Artist on Staff

Ryan Davis
Graphic Designer

Blake Benda
Custom publishing | Retail Liaison
Sales Representative
BBenda@Ape-Entertainment.com

Company Information:
Ape Entertainment
P.O. Box 212344
Chula Vista, CA 91921

For Advertising contact:
The Bonfire Agency
Ed Cato
ed.catto@bonfireagency.com
917.595.4107

Ape Entertainment Websites:
ApeComics.com
KiZoic.com

TWITTER:
Twitter.com/ApeComics

FACEBOOK:
Facebook.com/ApeEntertainment

YOUTUBE:
YouTube.com/user/ApeEntertainment

**To find more great comics,
visit us on the web at
KiZoic.com**

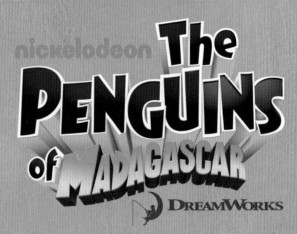

"OPERATION: WEAKEST LINK"
WRITER- DAVE SERVER & JACKSON LANZING
ARTIST- ANTONIO CAMPO COLORS- DIEGO RODRIGUEZ
LETTERS- DERON BENNETT

"RICO'S BAD DAY"
WRITER- DAVE SERVER & JACKSON LANZING
ARTIST- BOB RENZAS COLORS- ALEKSANDR DE PAYEVSKY
LETTERS- DERON BENNETT

"IT'S A MAN'S WORLD"
WRITER- DAVE SERVER & JACKSON LANZING
ARTIST- ANTONIO CAMPO COLORS- DIEGO RODRIGUEZ
LETTERS- DERON BENNETT

"SUBWAY SHENANIGANS"
WRITER- DAVE SERVER & JACKSON LANZING
ARTIST- JAMES SILVANI COLORS- DIEGO RODRIGUEZ
LETTERS- DERON BENNETT

OPERATION: WEAKEST LINK

Written by David Server & Jackson Lanzing
Art by Antonio Campo • Colors by Diego Rodriguez
Letters by Deron Bennett • Edited by Aaron Sparrow

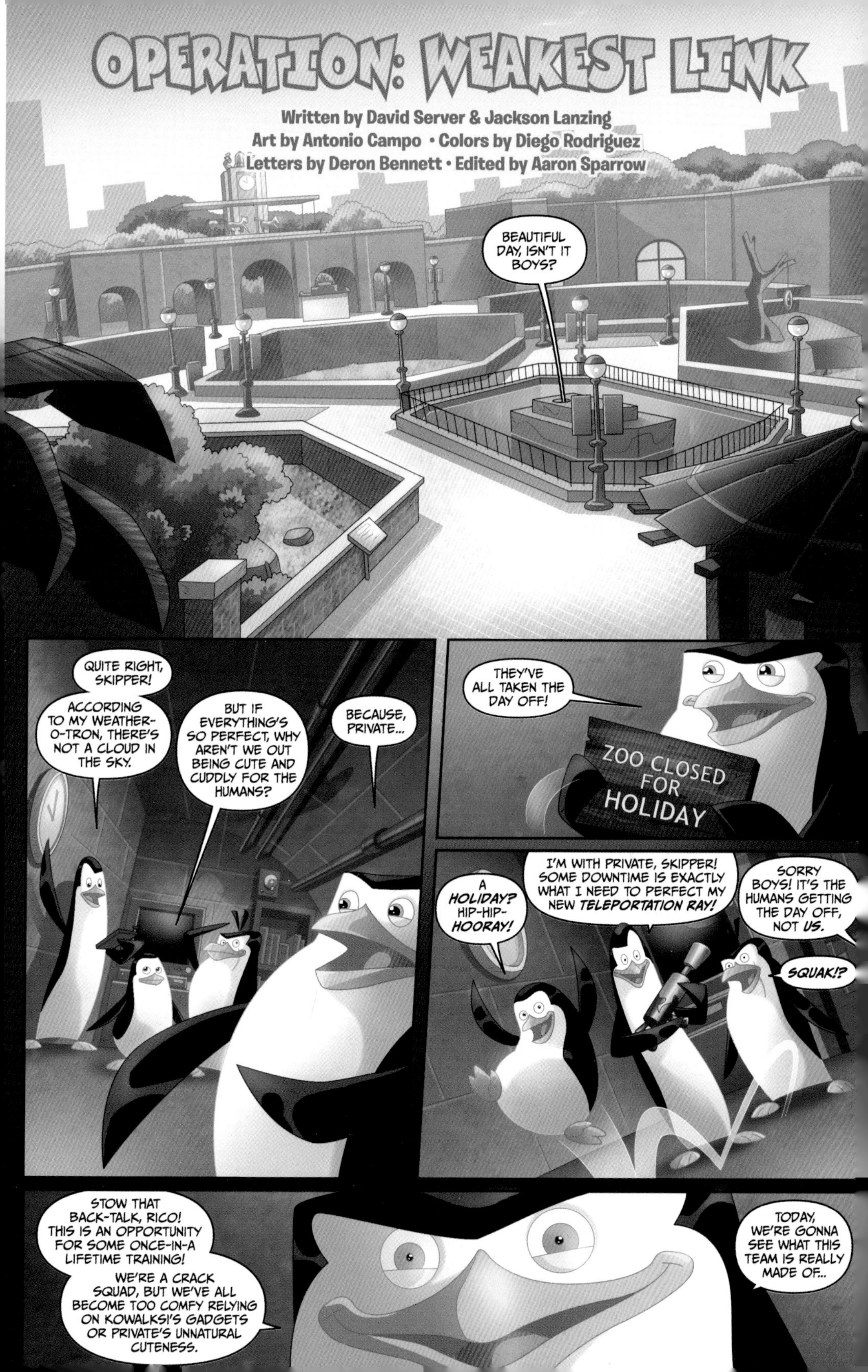

BEAUTIFUL DAY, ISN'T IT BOYS?
QUITE RIGHT, SKIPPER!
ACCORDING TO MY WEATHER-O-TRON, THERE'S NOT A CLOUD IN THE SKY.
BUT IF EVERYTHING'S SO PERFECT, WHY AREN'T WE OUT BEING CUTE AND CUDDLY FOR THE HUMANS?
BECAUSE, PRIVATE...
THEY'VE ALL TAKEN THE DAY OFF!
ZOO CLOSED FOR HOLIDAY
A *HOLIDAY?* HIP-HIP-*HOORAY!*
I'M WITH PRIVATE, SKIPPER! SOME DOWNTIME IS EXACTLY WHAT I NEED TO PERFECT MY NEW *TELEPORTATION RAY!*
SORRY BOYS! IT'S THE HUMANS GETTING THE DAY OFF, NOT *US*.
SQUAK!?
STOW THAT BACK-TALK, RICO! THIS IS AN OPPORTUNITY FOR SOME ONCE-IN-A LIFETIME TRAINING!
WE'RE A CRACK SQUAD, BUT WE'VE ALL BECOME TOO COMFY RELYING ON KOWALKSI'S GADGETS OR PRIVATE'S UNNATURAL CUTENESS.
TODAY, WE'RE GONNA SEE WHAT THIS TEAM IS REALLY MADE OF...

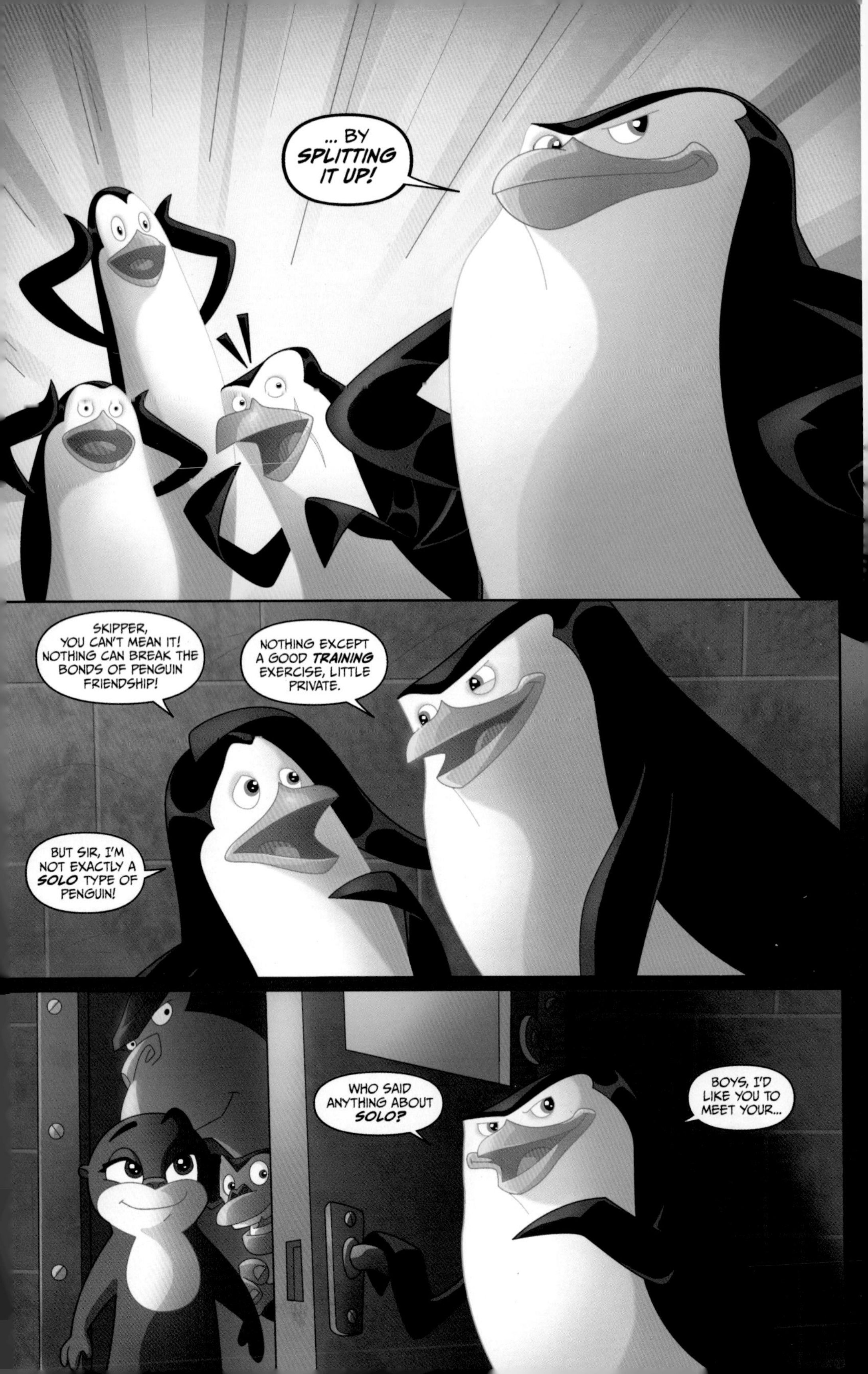
... BY SPLITTING IT UP!
SKIPPER, YOU CAN'T MEAN IT! NOTHING CAN BREAK THE BONDS OF PENGUIN FRIENDSHIP!
NOTHING EXCEPT A GOOD TRAINING EXERCISE, LITTLE PRIVATE.
BUT SIR, I'M NOT EXACTLY A SOLO TYPE OF PENGUIN!
WHO SAID ANYTHING ABOUT SOLO?
BOYS, I'D LIKE YOU TO MEET YOUR...

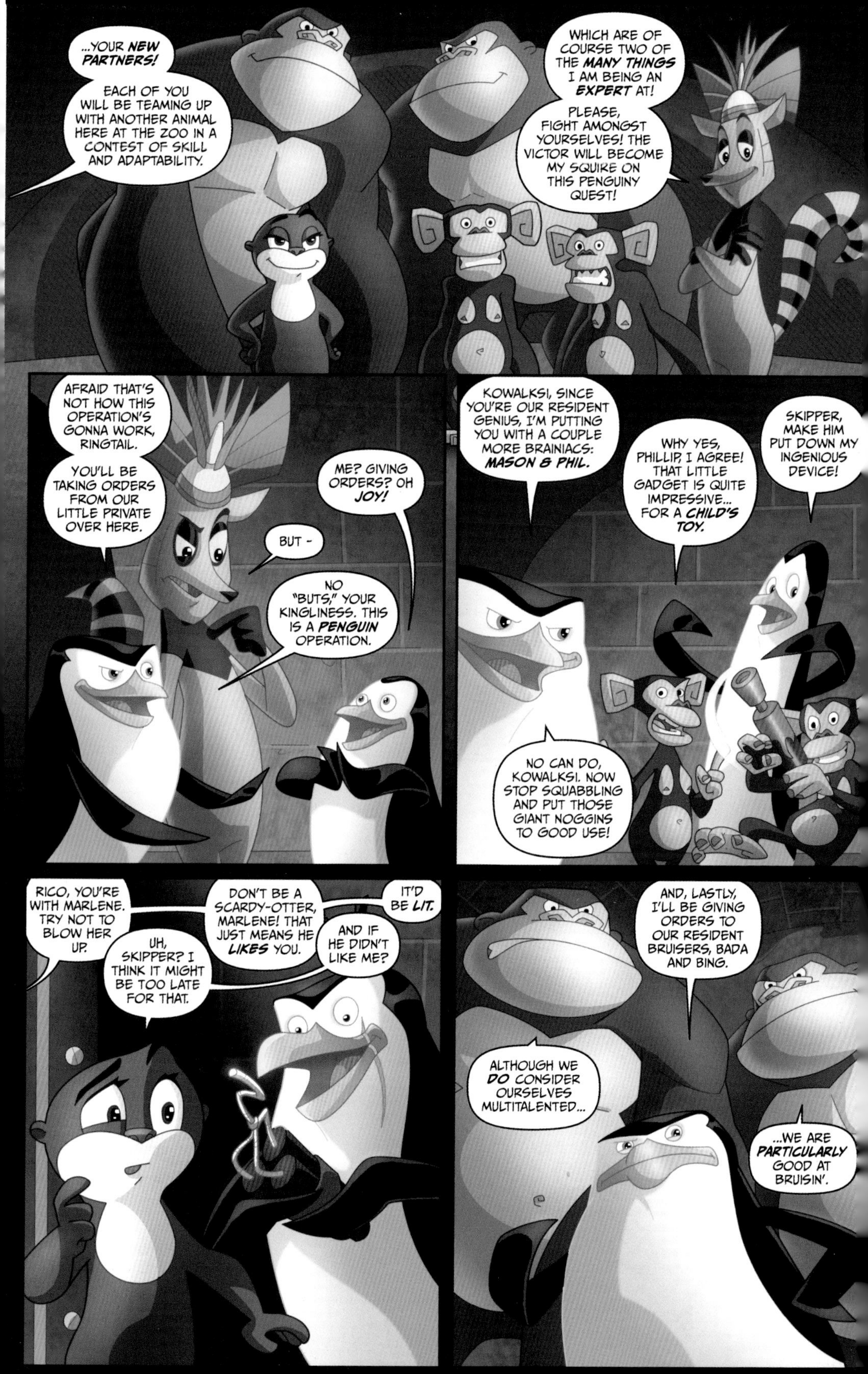
...YOUR *NEW PARTNERS!*
EACH OF YOU WILL BE TEAMING UP WITH ANOTHER ANIMAL HERE AT THE ZOO IN A CONTEST OF SKILL AND ADAPTABILITY.
WHICH ARE OF COURSE TWO OF THE *MANY THINGS* I AM BEING AN *EXPERT* AT!
PLEASE, FIGHT AMONGST YOURSELVES! THE VICTOR WILL BECOME MY SQUIRE ON THIS PENGUINY QUEST!
AFRAID THAT'S NOT HOW THIS OPERATION'S GONNA WORK, RINGTAIL.
YOU'LL BE TAKING ORDERS FROM OUR LITTLE PRIVATE OVER HERE.
ME? GIVING ORDERS? OH *JOY!*
BUT -
NO "BUTS," YOUR KINGLINESS. THIS IS A *PENGUIN* OPERATION.
KOWALKSI, SINCE YOU'RE OUR RESIDENT GENIUS, I'M PUTTING YOU WITH A COUPLE MORE BRAINIACS: *MASON & PHIL.*
WHY YES, PHILLIP, I AGREE! THAT LITTLE GADGET IS QUITE IMPRESSIVE... FOR A *CHILD'S TOY.*
SKIPPER, MAKE HIM PUT DOWN MY INGENIOUS DEVICE!
NO CAN DO, KOWALKSI. NOW STOP SQUABBLING AND PUT THOSE GIANT NOGGINS TO GOOD USE!
RICO, YOU'RE WITH MARLENE. TRY NOT TO BLOW HER UP.
UH, SKIPPER? I THINK IT MIGHT BE TOO LATE FOR THAT.
DON'T BE A SCARDY-OTTER, MARLENE! THAT JUST MEANS HE *LIKES* YOU.
AND IF HE DIDN'T LIKE ME?
IT'D BE *LIT.*
AND, LASTLY, I'LL BE GIVING ORDERS TO OUR RESIDENT BRUISERS, BADA AND BING.
ALTHOUGH WE *DO* CONSIDER OURSELVES MULTITALENTED...
...WE ARE *PARTICULARLY* GOOD AT BRUISIN'.

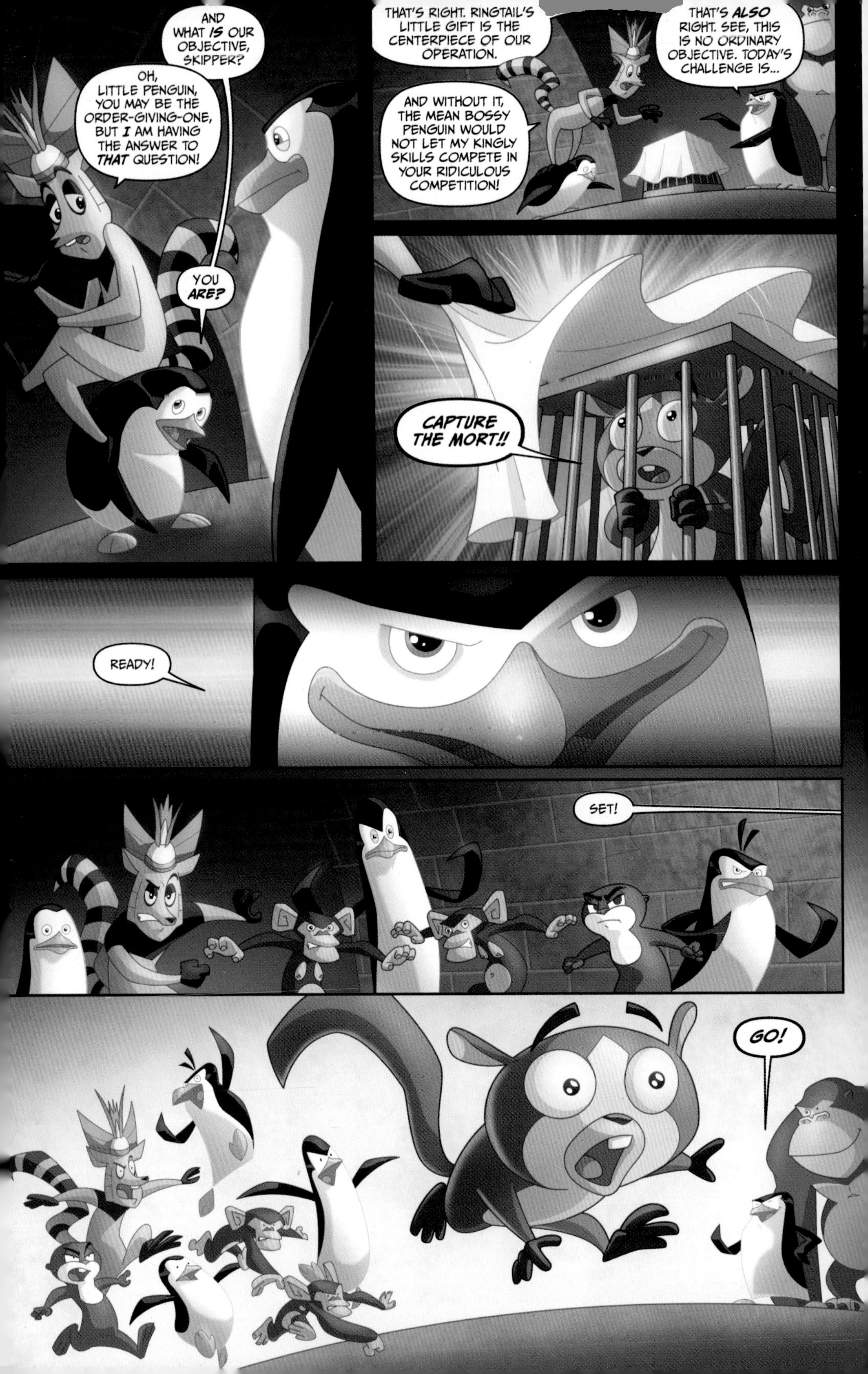
AND WHAT IS OUR OBJECTIVE, SKIPPER?
OH, LITTLE PENGUIN, YOU MAY BE THE ORDER-GIVING-ONE, BUT I AM HAVING THE ANSWER TO THAT QUESTION!
YOU ARE?
THAT'S RIGHT. RINGTAIL'S LITTLE GIFT IS THE CENTERPIECE OF OUR OPERATION.
AND WITHOUT IT, THE MEAN BOSSY PENGUIN WOULD NOT LET MY KINGLY SKILLS COMPETE IN YOUR RIDICULOUS COMPETITION!
THAT'S ALSO RIGHT. SEE, THIS IS NO ORDINARY OBJECTIVE. TODAY'S CHALLENGE IS...
CAPTURE THE MORT!!
READY!
SET!
GO!

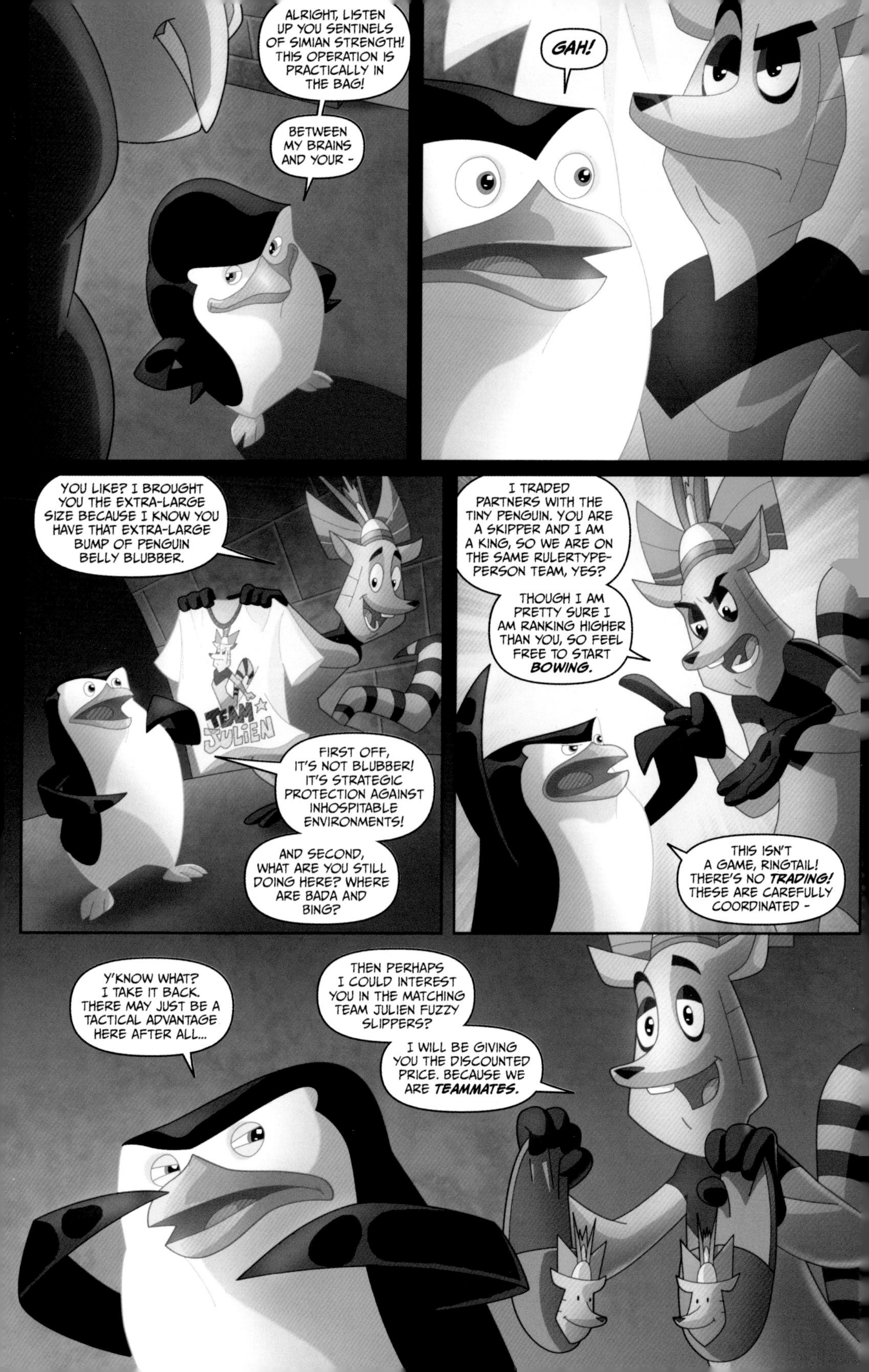

ALRIGHT, LISTEN UP YOU SENTINELS OF SIMIAN STRENGTH! THIS OPERATION IS PRACTICALLY IN THE BAG!
BETWEEN MY BRAINS AND YOUR -
GAH!
YOU LIKE? I BROUGHT YOU THE EXTRA-LARGE SIZE BECAUSE I KNOW YOU HAVE THAT EXTRA-LARGE BUMP OF PENGUIN BELLY BLUBBER.
TEAM JULIEN
FIRST OFF, IT'S NOT BLUBBER! IT'S STRATEGIC PROTECTION AGAINST INHOSPITABLE ENVIRONMENTS!
AND SECOND, WHAT ARE YOU STILL DOING HERE? WHERE ARE BADA AND BING?
I TRADED PARTNERS WITH THE TINY PENGUIN. YOU ARE A SKIPPER AND I AM A KING, SO WE ARE ON THE SAME RULERTYPE-PERSON TEAM, YES?
THOUGH I AM PRETTY SURE I AM RANKING HIGHER THAN YOU, SO FEEL FREE TO START ***BOWING.***
THIS ISN'T A GAME, RINGTAIL! THERE'S NO ***TRADING!*** THESE ARE CAREFULLY COORDINATED -
Y'KNOW WHAT? I TAKE IT BACK. THERE MAY JUST BE A TACTICAL ADVANTAGE HERE AFTER ALL...
THEN PERHAPS I COULD INTEREST YOU IN THE MATCHING TEAM JULIEN FUZZY SLIPPERS?
I WILL BE GIVING YOU THE DISCOUNTED PRICE. BECAUSE WE ARE ***TEAMMATES.***

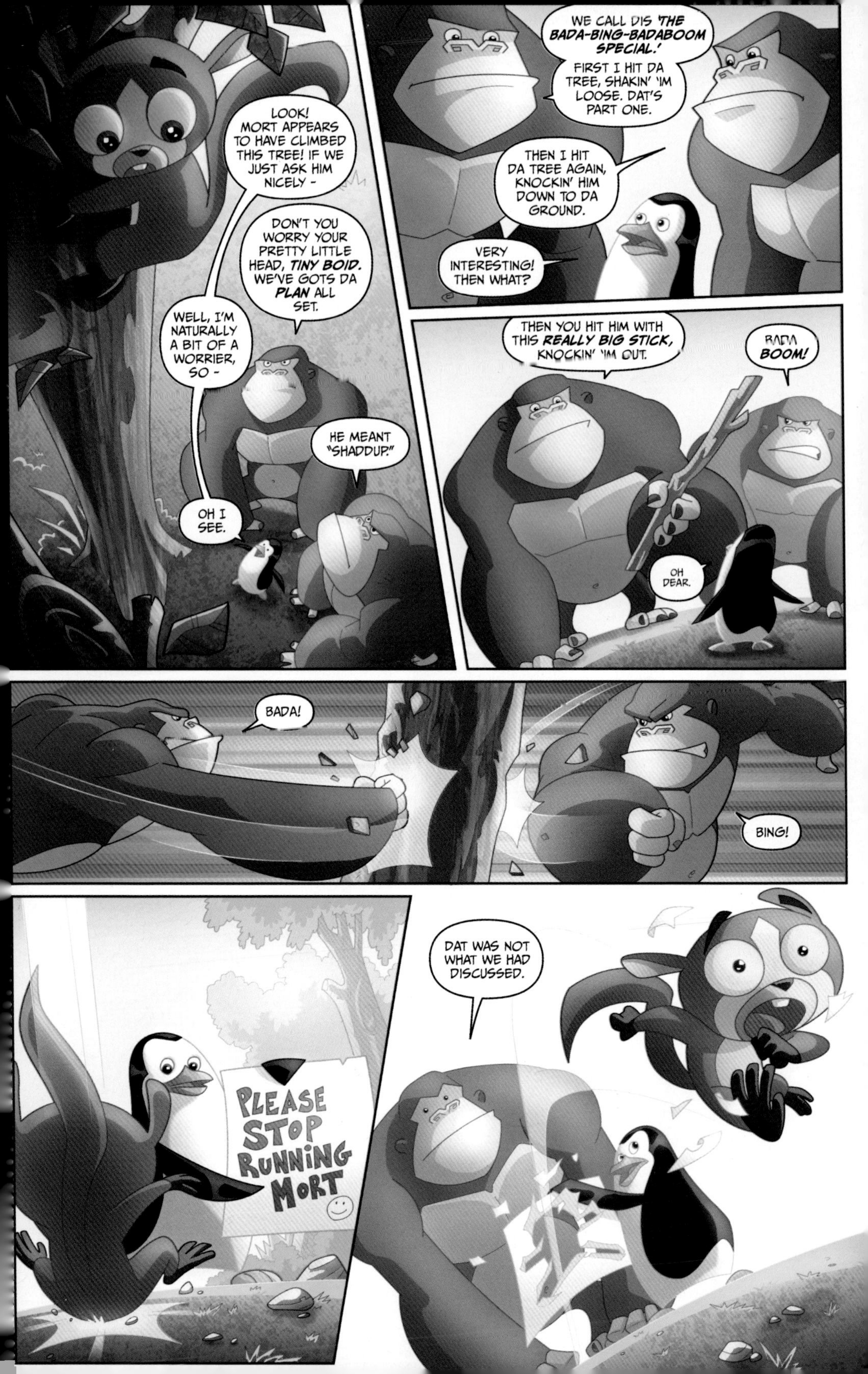
LOOK! MORT APPEARS TO HAVE CLIMBED THIS TREE! IF WE JUST ASK HIM NICELY -
DON'T YOU WORRY YOUR PRETTY LITTLE HEAD, TINY BOID. WE'VE GOTS DA PLAN ALL SET.
WELL, I'M NATURALLY A BIT OF A WORRIER, SO -
HE MEANT "SHADDUP."
OH I SEE.
WE CALL DIS 'THE BADA-BING-BADABOOM SPECIAL.'
FIRST I HIT DA TREE, SHAKIN' 'IM LOOSE. DAT'S PART ONE.
THEN I HIT DA TREE AGAIN, KNOCKIN' HIM DOWN TO DA GROUND.
VERY INTERESTING! THEN WHAT?
THEN YOU HIT HIM WITH THIS REALLY BIG STICK, KNOCKIN' 'IM OUT.
BADA BOOM!
OH DEAR.
BADA!
BING!
DAT WAS NOT WHAT WE HAD DISCUSSED.
PLEASE STOP RUNNING MORT

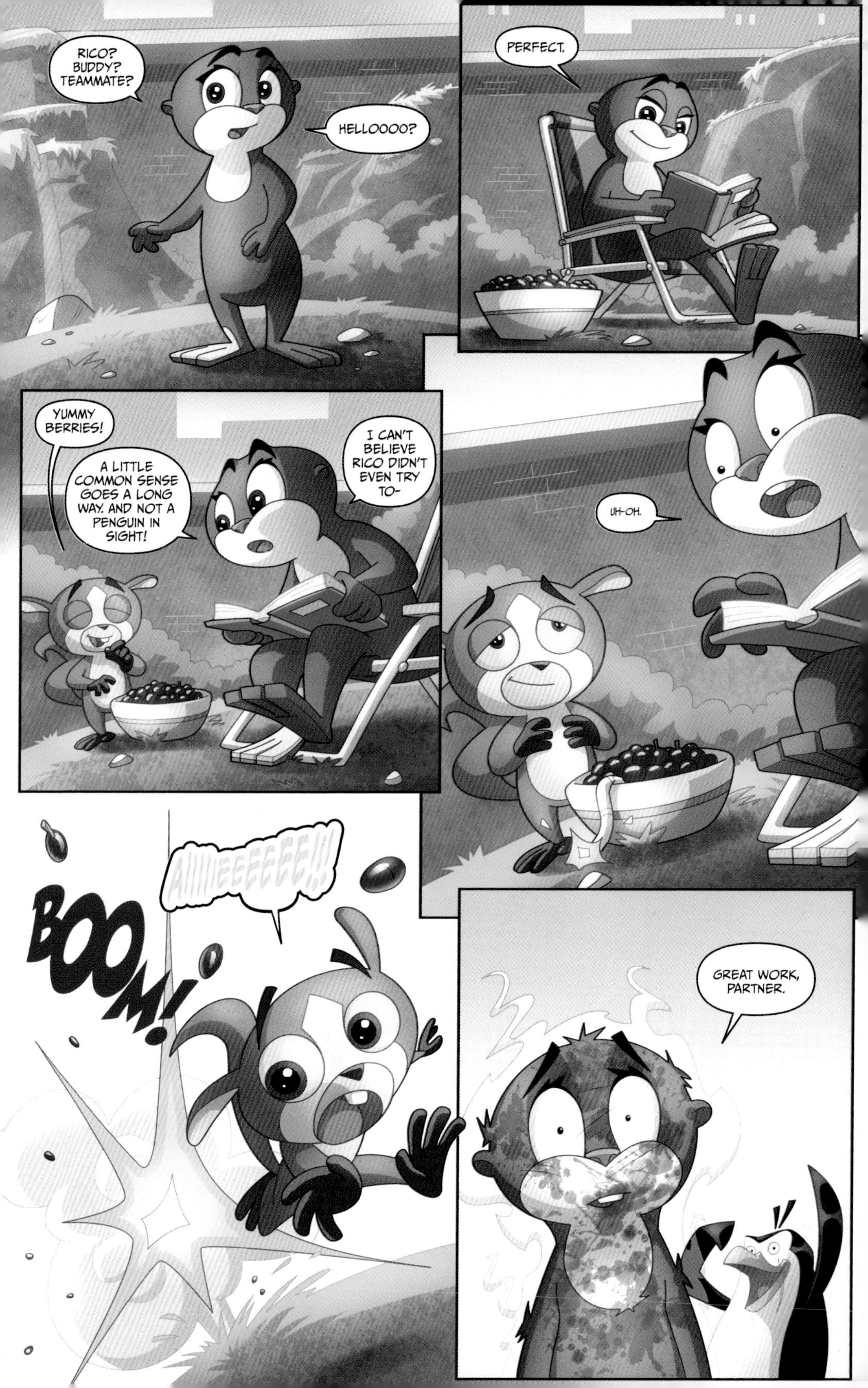
RICO? BUDDY? TEAMMATE?
HELLOOOO?
PERFECT.
YUMMY BERRIES!
A LITTLE COMMON SENSE GOES A LONG WAY. AND NOT A PENGUIN IN SIGHT!
I CAN'T BELIEVE RICO DIDN'T EVEN TRY TO-
UH-OH.
BOOM!
AIIIIEEEEEEE!!!
GREAT WORK, PARTNER.

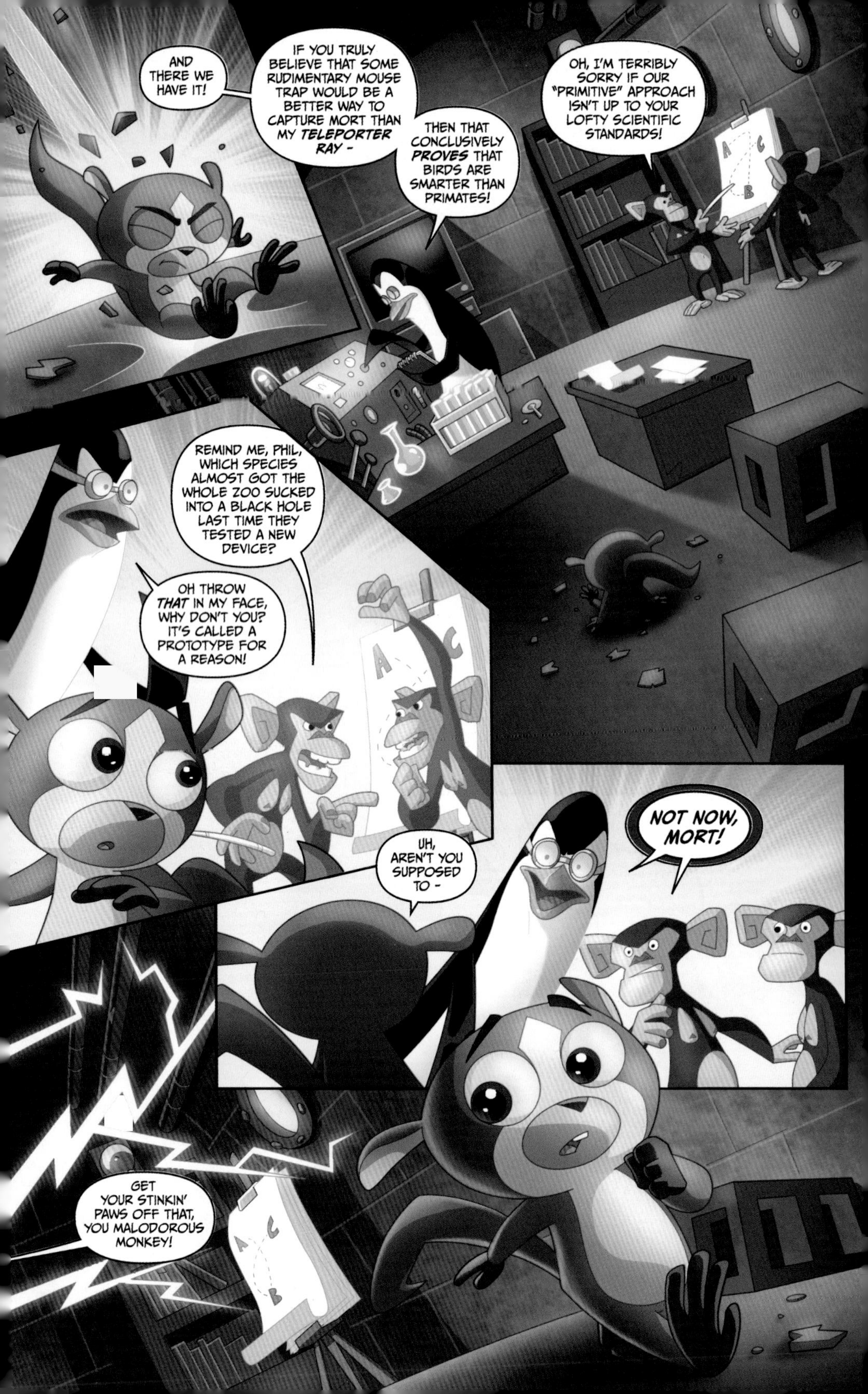
AND THERE WE HAVE IT!
IF YOU TRULY BELIEVE THAT SOME RUDIMENTARY MOUSE TRAP WOULD BE A BETTER WAY TO CAPTURE MORT THAN MY *TELEPORTER RAY* -
THEN THAT CONCLUSIVELY *PROVES* THAT BIRDS ARE SMARTER THAN PRIMATES!
OH, I'M TERRIBLY SORRY IF OUR "PRIMITIVE" APPROACH ISN'T UP TO YOUR LOFTY SCIENTIFIC STANDARDS!
REMIND ME, PHIL, WHICH SPECIES ALMOST GOT THE WHOLE ZOO SUCKED INTO A BLACK HOLE LAST TIME THEY TESTED A NEW DEVICE?
OH THROW *THAT* IN MY FACE, WHY DON'T YOU? IT'S CALLED A PROTOTYPE FOR A REASON!
UH, AREN'T YOU SUPPOSED TO -
NOT NOW, MORT!
GET YOUR STINKIN' PAWS OFF THAT, YOU MALODOROUS MONKEY!

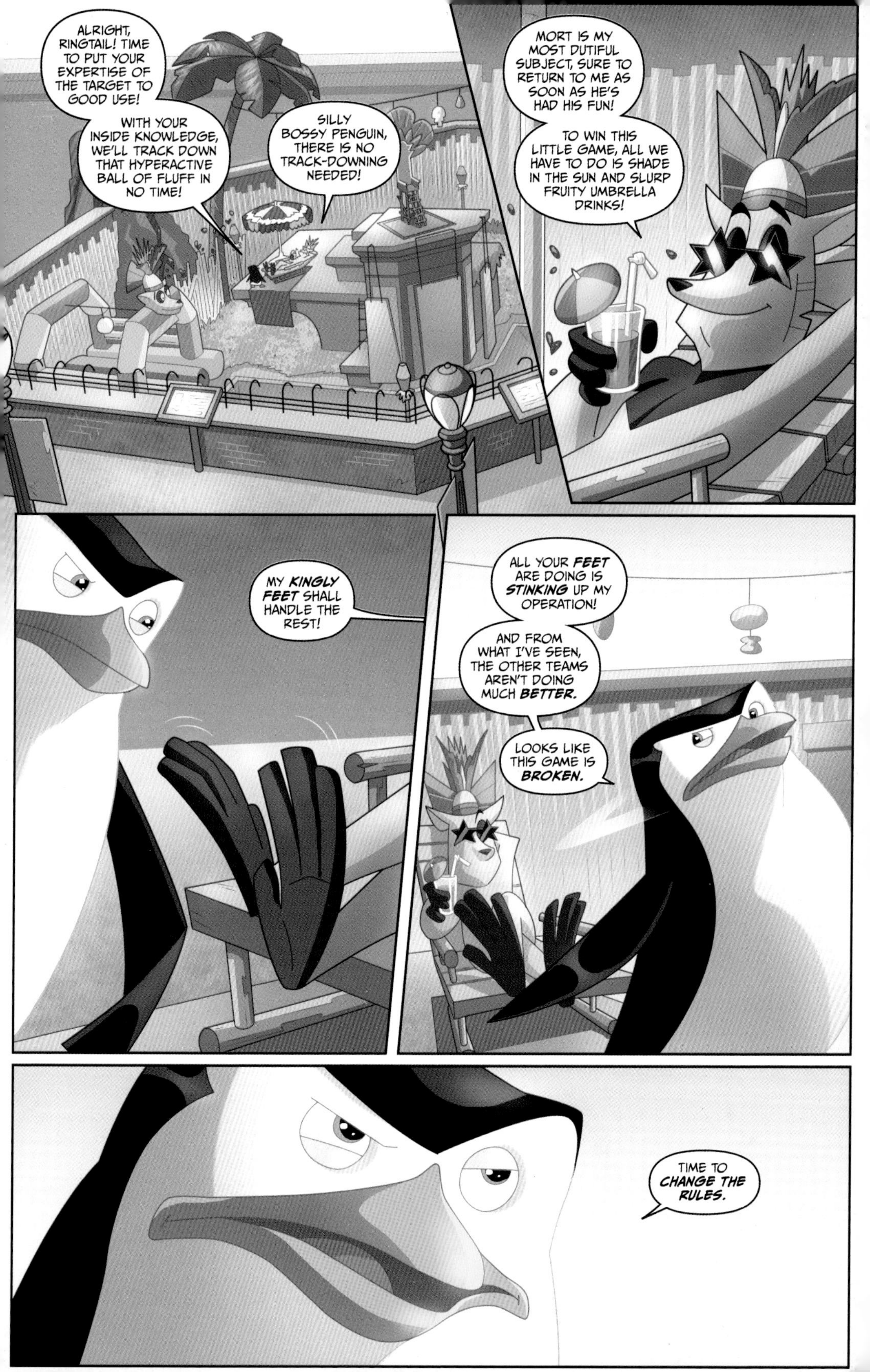
ALRIGHT, RINGTAIL! TIME TO PUT YOUR EXPERTISE OF THE TARGET TO GOOD USE!
WITH YOUR INSIDE KNOWLEDGE, WE'LL TRACK DOWN THAT HYPERACTIVE BALL OF FLUFF IN NO TIME!
SILLY BOSSY PENGUIN, THERE IS NO TRACK-DOWNING NEEDED!
MORT IS MY MOST DUTIFUL SUBJECT, SURE TO RETURN TO ME AS SOON AS HE'S HAD HIS FUN!
TO WIN THIS LITTLE GAME, ALL WE HAVE TO DO IS SHADE IN THE SUN AND SLURP FRUITY UMBRELLA DRINKS!
MY KINGLY FEET SHALL HANDLE THE REST!
ALL YOUR FEET ARE DOING IS STINKING UP MY OPERATION!
AND FROM WHAT I'VE SEEN, THE OTHER TEAMS AREN'T DOING MUCH BETTER.
LOOKS LIKE THIS GAME IS BROKEN.
TIME TO CHANGE THE RULES.

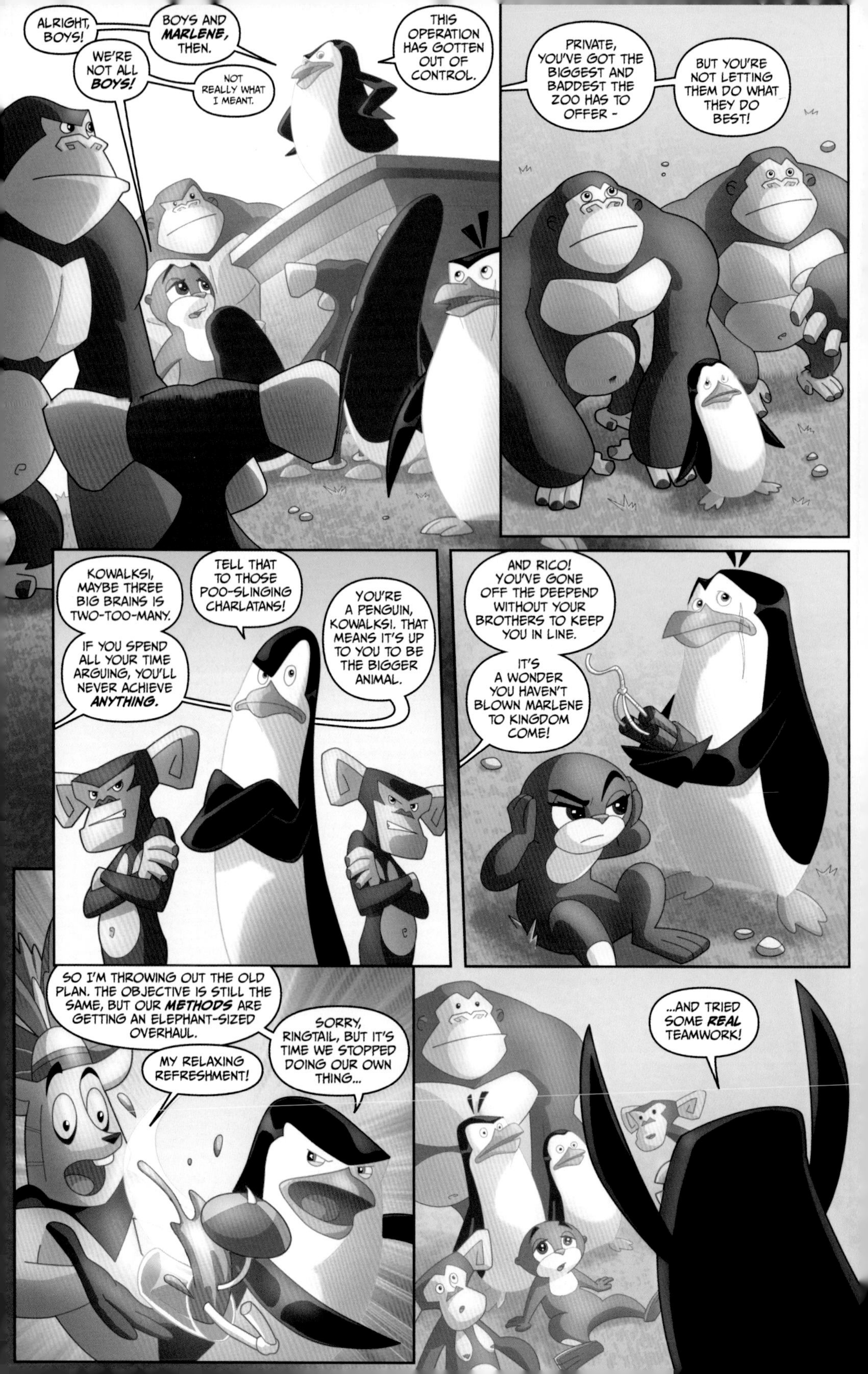
ALRIGHT, BOYS!
BOYS AND *MARLENE,* THEN.
WE'RE NOT ALL *BOYS!*
NOT REALLY WHAT I MEANT.
THIS OPERATION HAS GOTTEN OUT OF CONTROL.
PRIVATE, YOU'VE GOT THE BIGGEST AND BADDEST THE ZOO HAS TO OFFER -
BUT YOU'RE NOT LETTING THEM DO WHAT THEY DO BEST!
KOWALKSI, MAYBE THREE BIG BRAINS IS TWO-TOO-MANY.
TELL THAT TO THOSE POO-SLINGING CHARLATANS!
IF YOU SPEND ALL YOUR TIME ARGUING, YOU'LL NEVER ACHIEVE *ANYTHING.*
YOU'RE A PENGUIN, KOWALKSI. THAT MEANS IT'S UP TO YOU TO BE THE BIGGER ANIMAL.
AND RICO! YOU'VE GONE OFF THE DEEPEND WITHOUT YOUR BROTHERS TO KEEP YOU IN LINE.
IT'S A WONDER YOU HAVEN'T BLOWN MARLENE TO KINGDOM COME!
SO I'M THROWING OUT THE OLD PLAN. THE OBJECTIVE IS STILL THE SAME, BUT OUR *METHODS* ARE GETTING AN ELEPHANT-SIZED OVERHAUL.
MY RELAXING REFRESHMENT!
SORRY, RINGTAIL, BUT IT'S TIME WE STOPPED DOING OUR OWN THING...
...AND TRIED SOME *REAL* TEAMWORK!

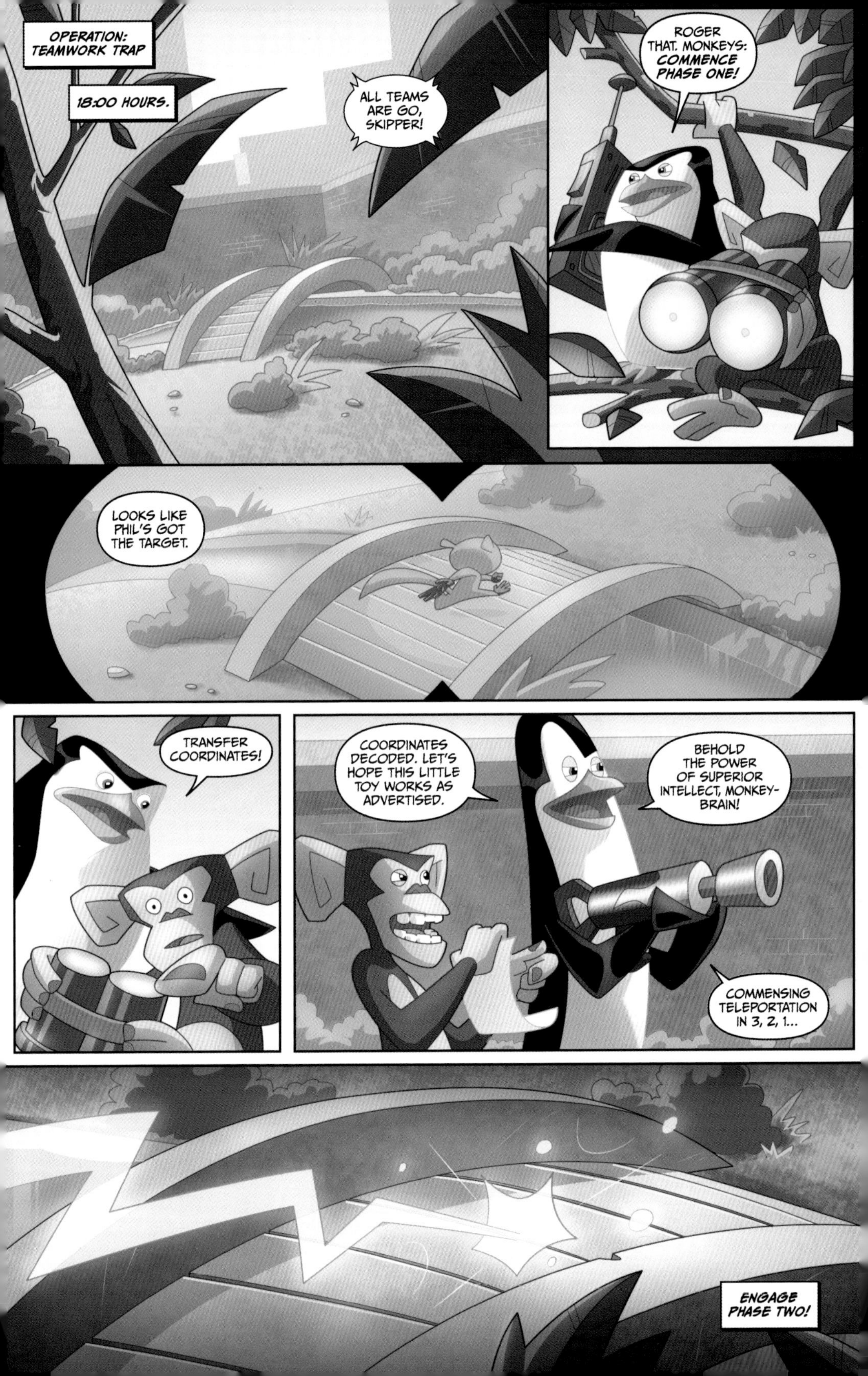
OPERATION: TEAMWORK TRAP
18:00 HOURS.
ALL TEAMS ARE GO, SKIPPER!
ROGER THAT. MONKEYS: COMMENCE PHASE ONE!
LOOKS LIKE PHIL'S GOT THE TARGET.
TRANSFER COORDINATES!
COORDINATES DECODED. LET'S HOPE THIS LITTLE TOY WORKS AS ADVERTISED.
BEHOLD THE POWER OF SUPERIOR INTELLECT, MONKEY-BRAIN!
COMMENSING TELEPORTATION IN 3, 2, 1...
ENGAGE PHASE TWO!

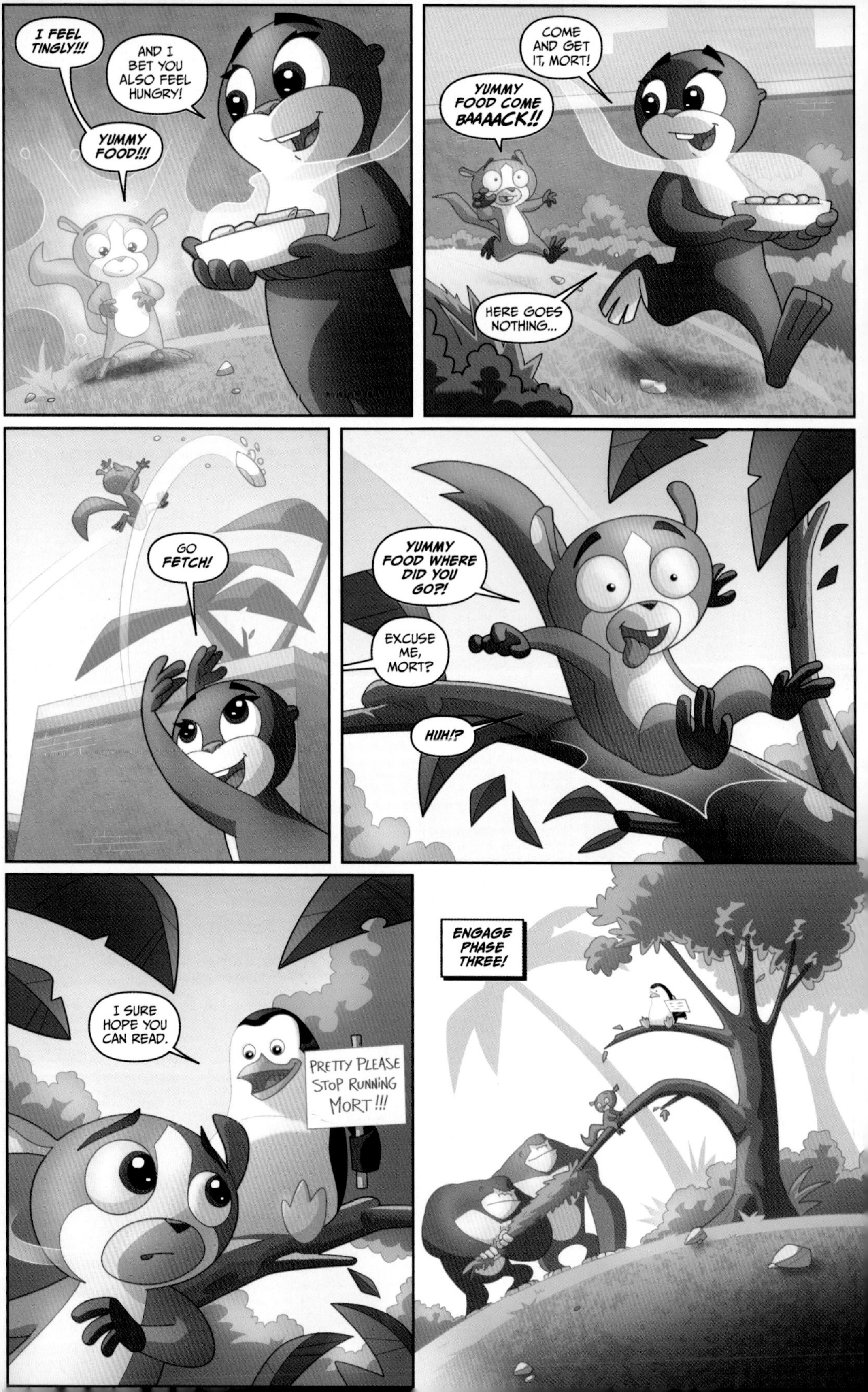

I FEEL TINGLY!!!
AND I BET YOU ALSO FEEL HUNGRY!
YUMMY FOOD!!!
COME AND GET IT, MORT!
YUMMY FOOD COME BAAAACK!!
HERE GOES NOTHING...
GO FETCH!
YUMMY FOOD WHERE DID YOU GO?!
EXCUSE ME, MORT?
HUH!?
I SURE HOPE YOU CAN READ.
PRETTY PLEASE STOP RUNNING MORT!!!
ENGAGE PHASE THREE!

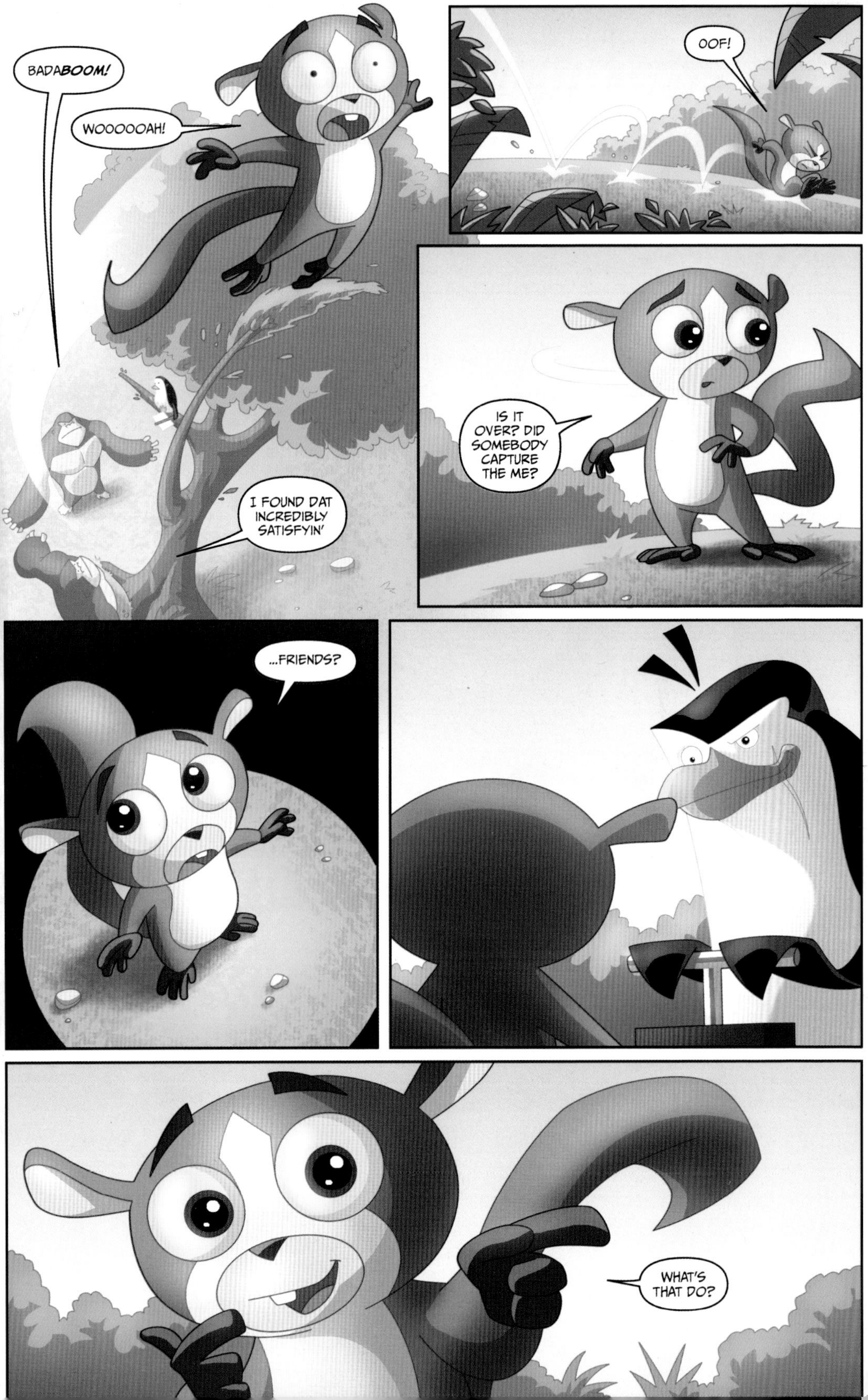
BADABOOM!
WOOOOOAH!
I FOUND DAT INCREDIBLY SATISFYIN'
OOF!
IS IT OVER? DID SOMEBODY CAPTURE THE ME?
...FRIENDS?
WHAT'S THAT DO?

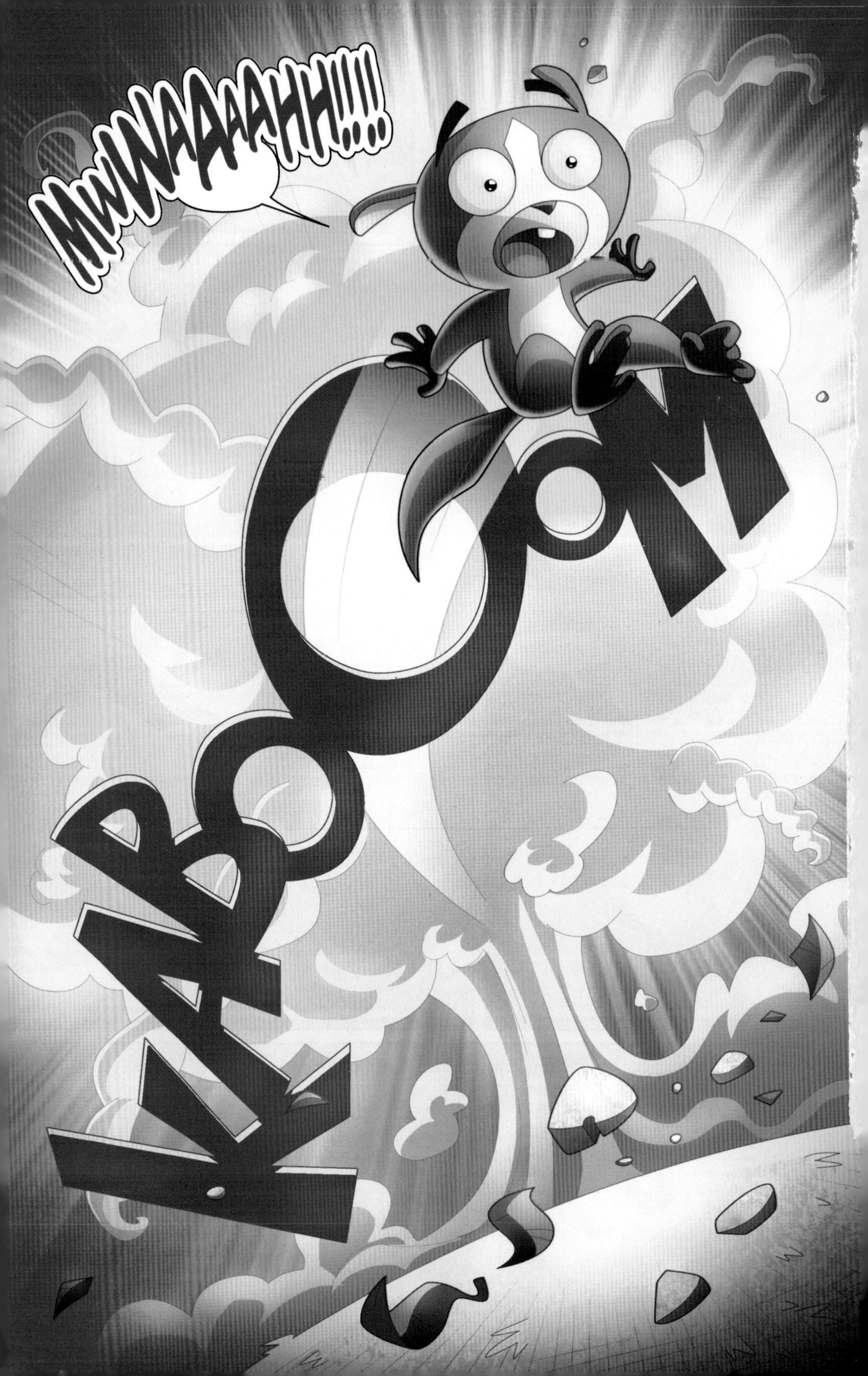
MWWAAAAHH!!!!
KABOOM

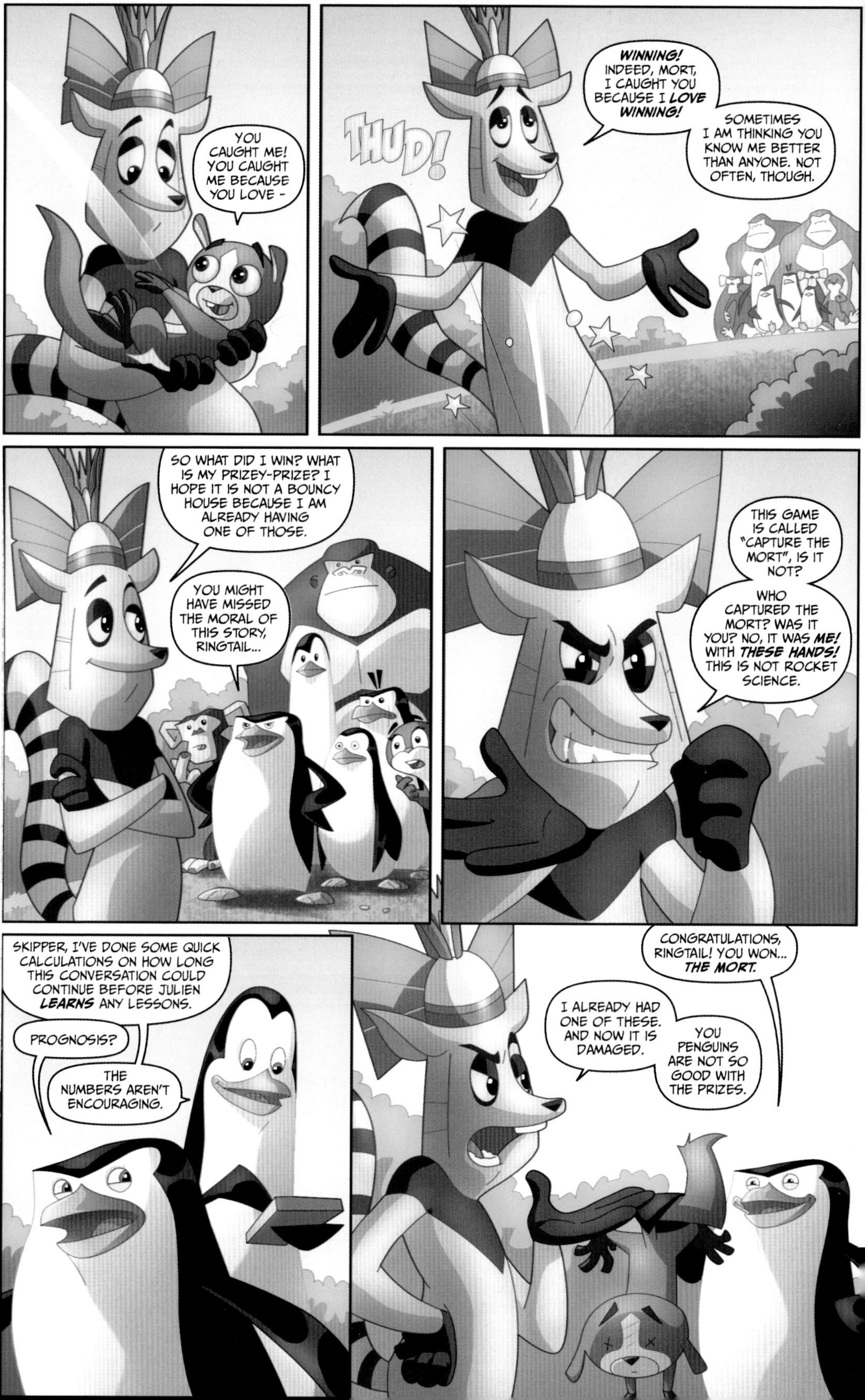
YOU CAUGHT ME! YOU CAUGHT ME BECAUSE YOU LOVE -
THUD!
WINNING! INDEED, MORT, I CAUGHT YOU BECAUSE I LOVE WINNING!
SOMETIMES I AM THINKING YOU KNOW ME BETTER THAN ANYONE. NOT OFTEN, THOUGH.
SO WHAT DID I WIN? WHAT IS MY PRIZEY-PRIZE? I HOPE IT IS NOT A BOUNCY HOUSE BECAUSE I AM ALREADY HAVING ONE OF THOSE.
YOU MIGHT HAVE MISSED THE MORAL OF THIS STORY, RINGTAIL...
THIS GAME IS CALLED "CAPTURE THE MORT", IS IT NOT?
WHO CAPTURED THE MORT? WAS IT YOU? NO, IT WAS ME! WITH THESE HANDS! THIS IS NOT ROCKET SCIENCE.
SKIPPER, I'VE DONE SOME QUICK CALCULATIONS ON HOW LONG THIS CONVERSATION COULD CONTINUE BEFORE JULIEN LEARNS ANY LESSONS.
PROGNOSIS?
THE NUMBERS AREN'T ENCOURAGING.
CONGRATULATIONS, RINGTAIL! YOU WON... THE MORT.
I ALREADY HAD ONE OF THESE. AND NOW IT IS DAMAGED.
YOU PENGUINS ARE NOT SO GOOD WITH THE PRIZES.

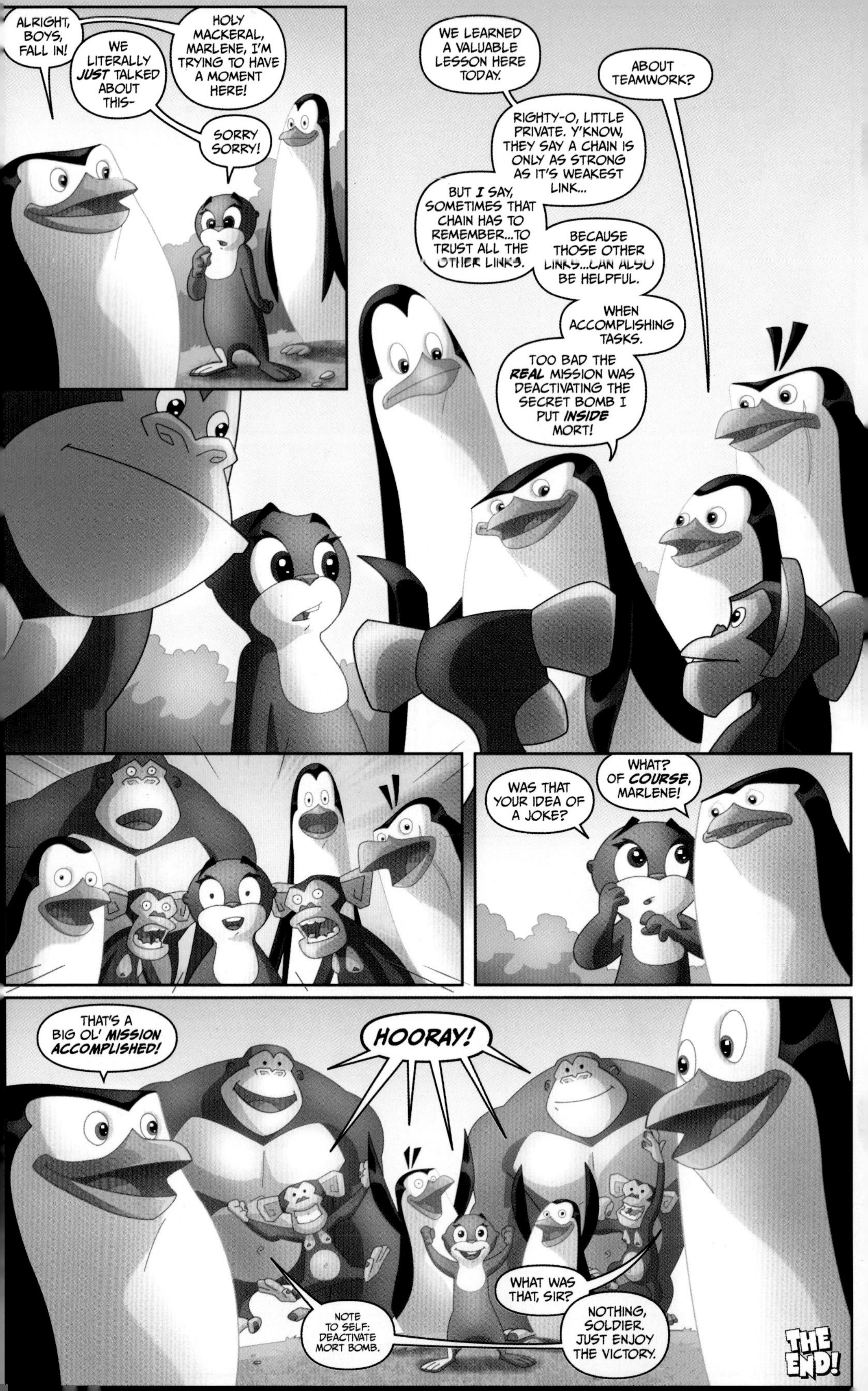
ALRIGHT, BOYS, FALL IN!
WE LITERALLY JUST TALKED ABOUT THIS-
HOLY MACKERAL, MARLENE, I'M TRYING TO HAVE A MOMENT HERE!
SORRY SORRY!
WE LEARNED A VALUABLE LESSON HERE TODAY.
ABOUT TEAMWORK?
RIGHTY-O, LITTLE PRIVATE. Y'KNOW, THEY SAY A CHAIN IS ONLY AS STRONG AS IT'S WEAKEST LINK...
BUT I SAY, SOMETIMES THAT CHAIN HAS TO REMEMBER...TO TRUST ALL THE OTHER LINKS.
BECAUSE THOSE OTHER LINKS...CAN ALSO BE HELPFUL.
WHEN ACCOMPLISHING TASKS.
TOO BAD THE REAL MISSION WAS DEACTIVATING THE SECRET BOMB I PUT INSIDE MORT!
WAS THAT YOUR IDEA OF A JOKE?
WHAT? OF COURSE, MARLENE!
THAT'S A BIG OL' MISSION ACCOMPLISHED!
HOORAY!
NOTE TO SELF: DEACTIVATE MORT BOMB.
WHAT WAS THAT, SIR?
NOTHING, SOLDIER. JUST ENJOY THE VICTORY.
THE END!

RICO'S BAD DAY

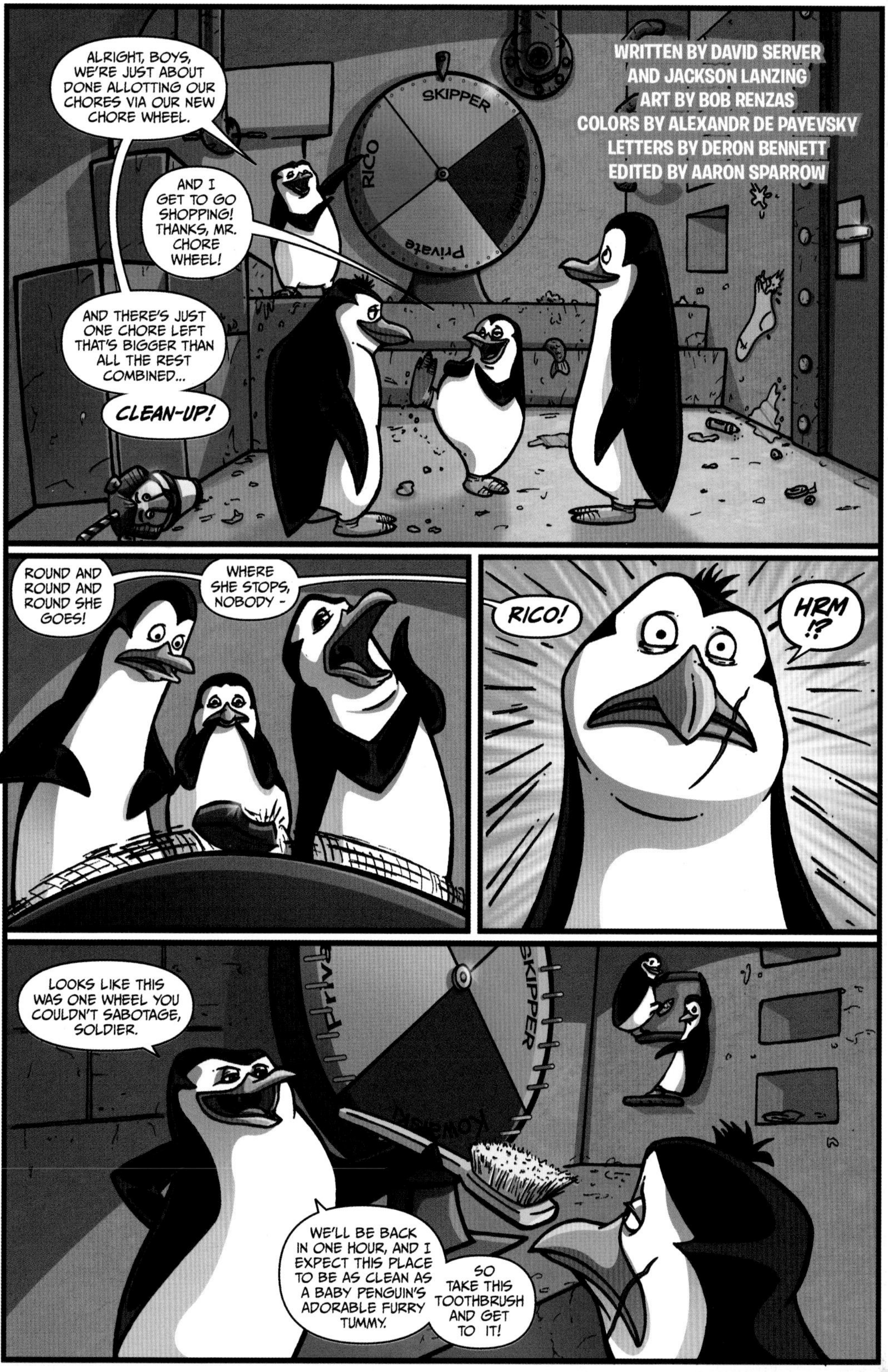
WRITTEN BY DAVID SERVER
AND JACKSON LANZING
ART BY BOB RENZAS
COLORS BY ALEXANDR DE PAYEVSKY
LETTERS BY DERON BENNETT
EDITED BY AARON SPARROW
SKIPPER
KOWALSKI
Private
RICO
ALRIGHT, BOYS, WE'RE JUST ABOUT DONE ALLOTTING OUR CHORES VIA OUR NEW CHORE WHEEL.
AND I GET TO GO SHOPPING! THANKS, MR. CHORE WHEEL!
AND THERE'S JUST ONE CHORE LEFT THAT'S BIGGER THAN ALL THE REST COMBINED...
CLEAN-UP!
ROUND AND ROUND AND ROUND SHE GOES!
WHERE SHE STOPS, NOBODY -
RICO!
HRM !?
LOOKS LIKE THIS WAS ONE WHEEL YOU COULDN'T SABOTAGE, SOLDIER.
WE'LL BE BACK IN ONE HOUR, AND I EXPECT THIS PLACE TO BE AS CLEAN AS A BABY PENGUIN'S ADORABLE FURRY TUMMY.
SO TAKE THIS TOOTHBRUSH AND GET TO IT!

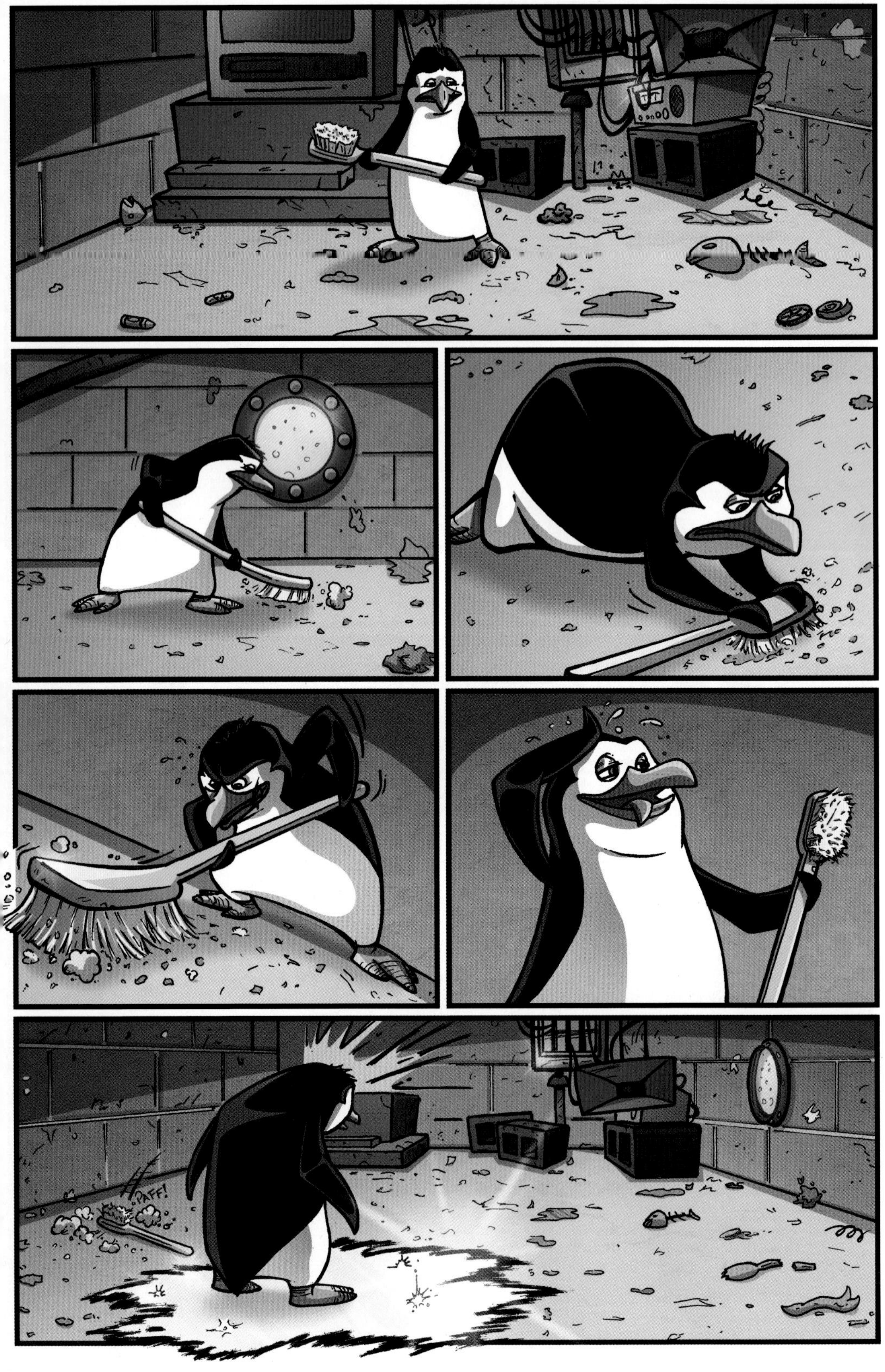
PAFF!

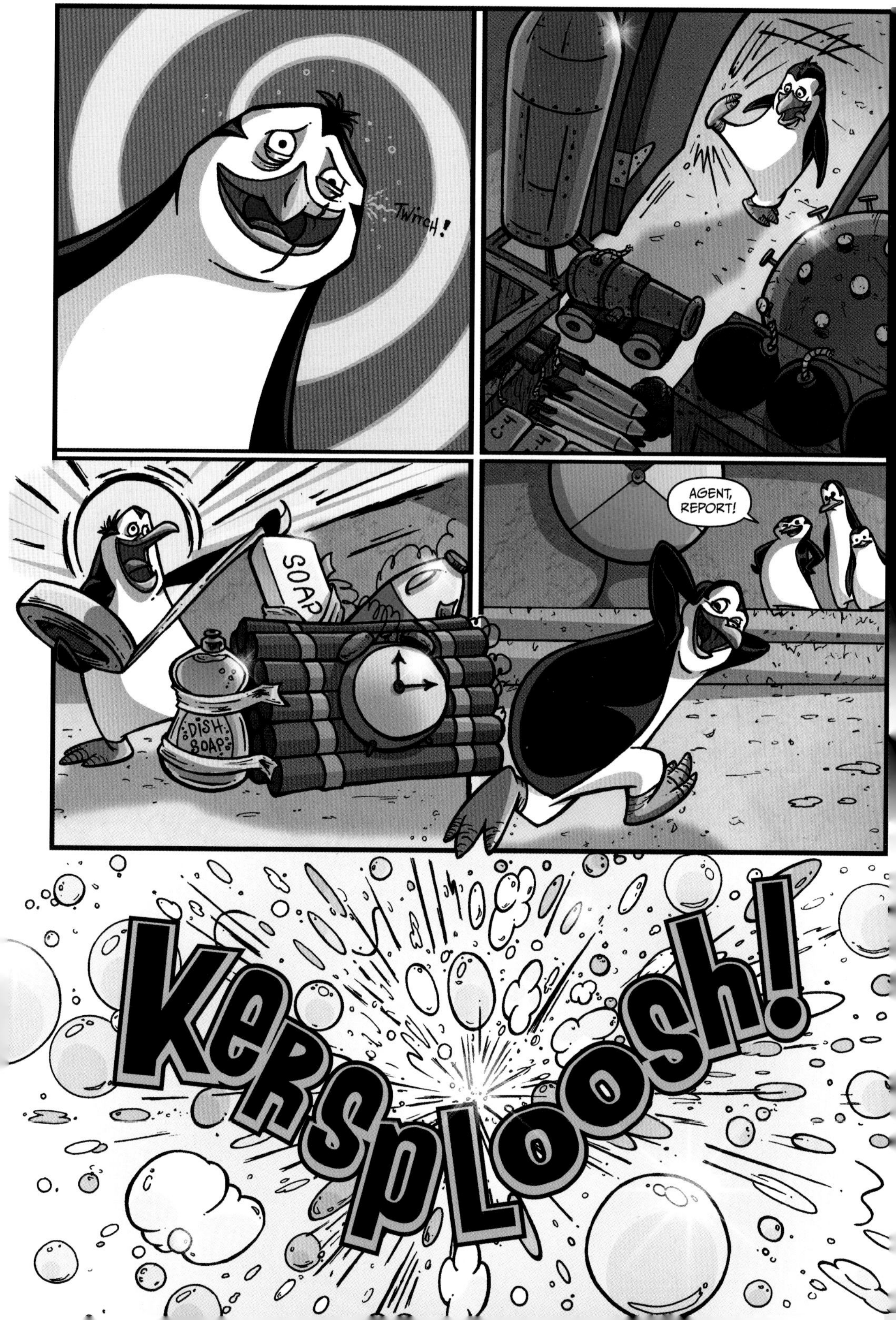
TWITCH!
SOAP
DISH SOAP
AGENT, REPORT!
KERSPLOOSH!

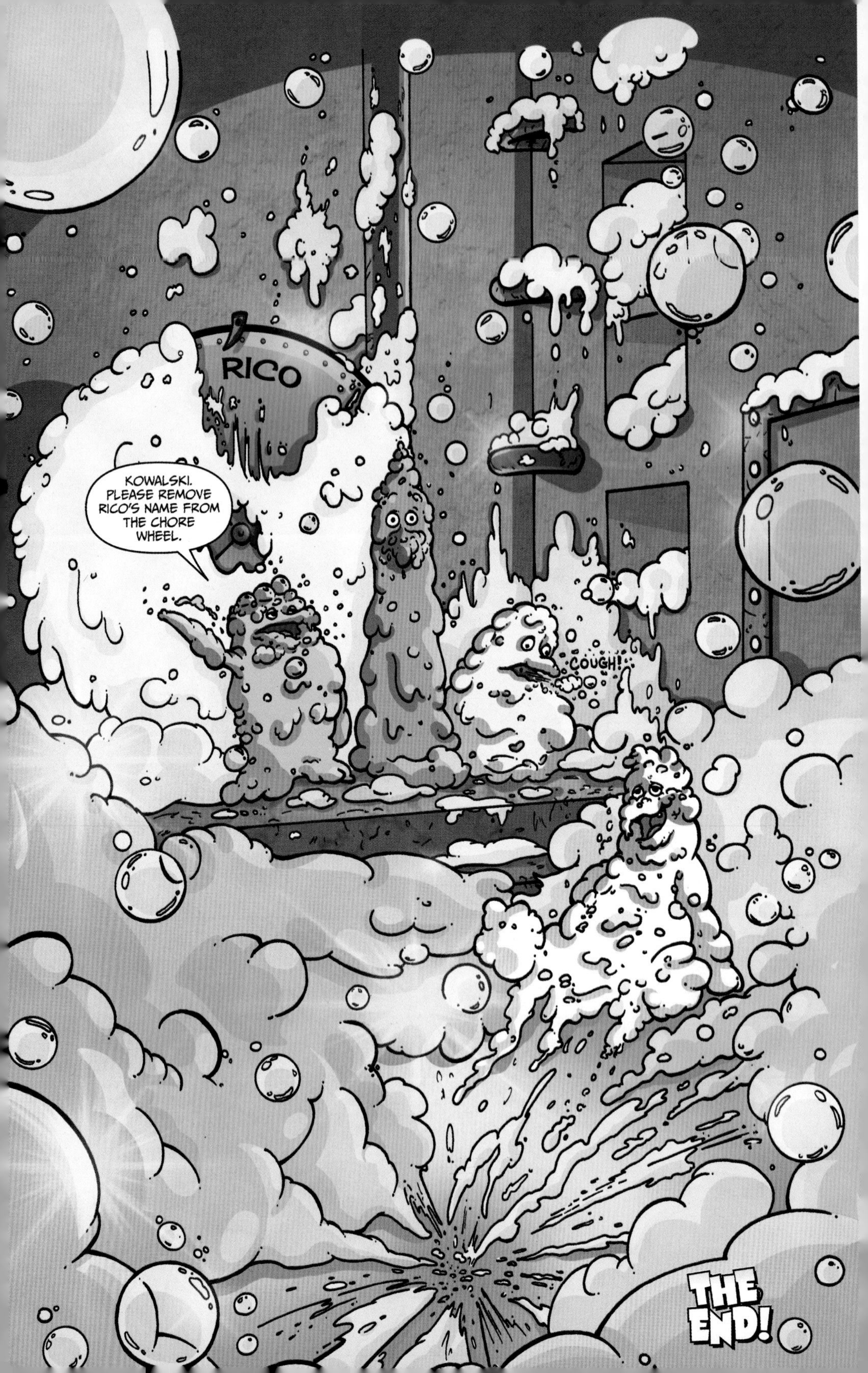
RICO
KOWALSKI. PLEASE REMOVE RICO'S NAME FROM THE CHORE WHEEL.
COUGH!
THE END!

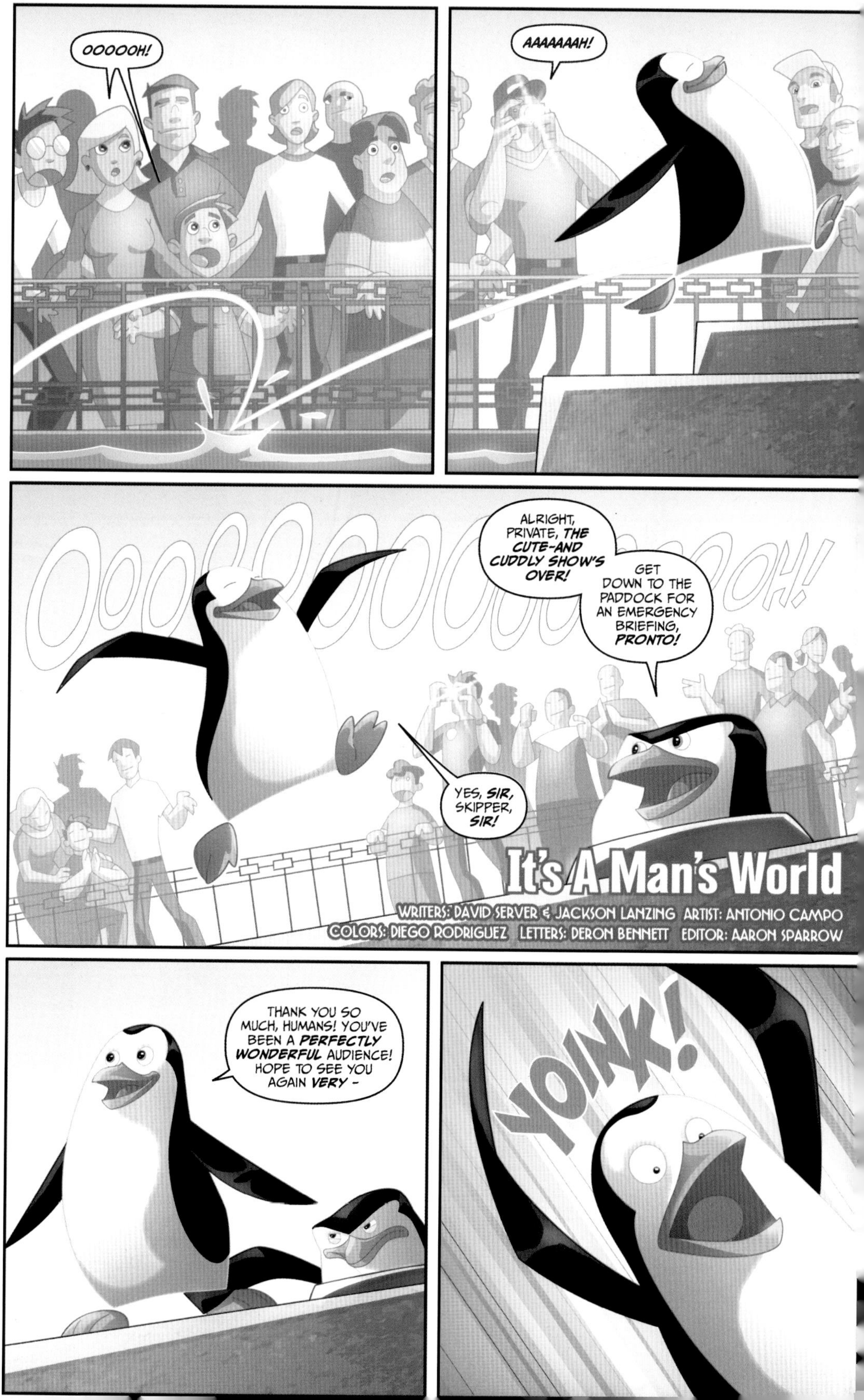
OOOOOH!
AAAAAAAH!
OOOOOOOOOOOOOOOOOOOH!
ALRIGHT, PRIVATE, THE CUTE-AND CUDDLY SHOW'S OVER!
GET DOWN TO THE PADDOCK FOR AN EMERGENCY BRIEFING, PRONTO!
YES, SIR, SKIPPER, SIR!
It's A Man's World
WRITERS: DAVID SERVER & JACKSON LANZING ARTIST: ANTONIO CAMPO
COLORS: DIEGO RODRIGUEZ LETTERS: DERON BENNETT EDITOR: AARON SPARROW
THANK YOU SO MUCH, HUMANS! YOU'VE BEEN A PERFECTLY WONDERFUL AUDIENCE! HOPE TO SEE YOU AGAIN VERY -
YOINK!

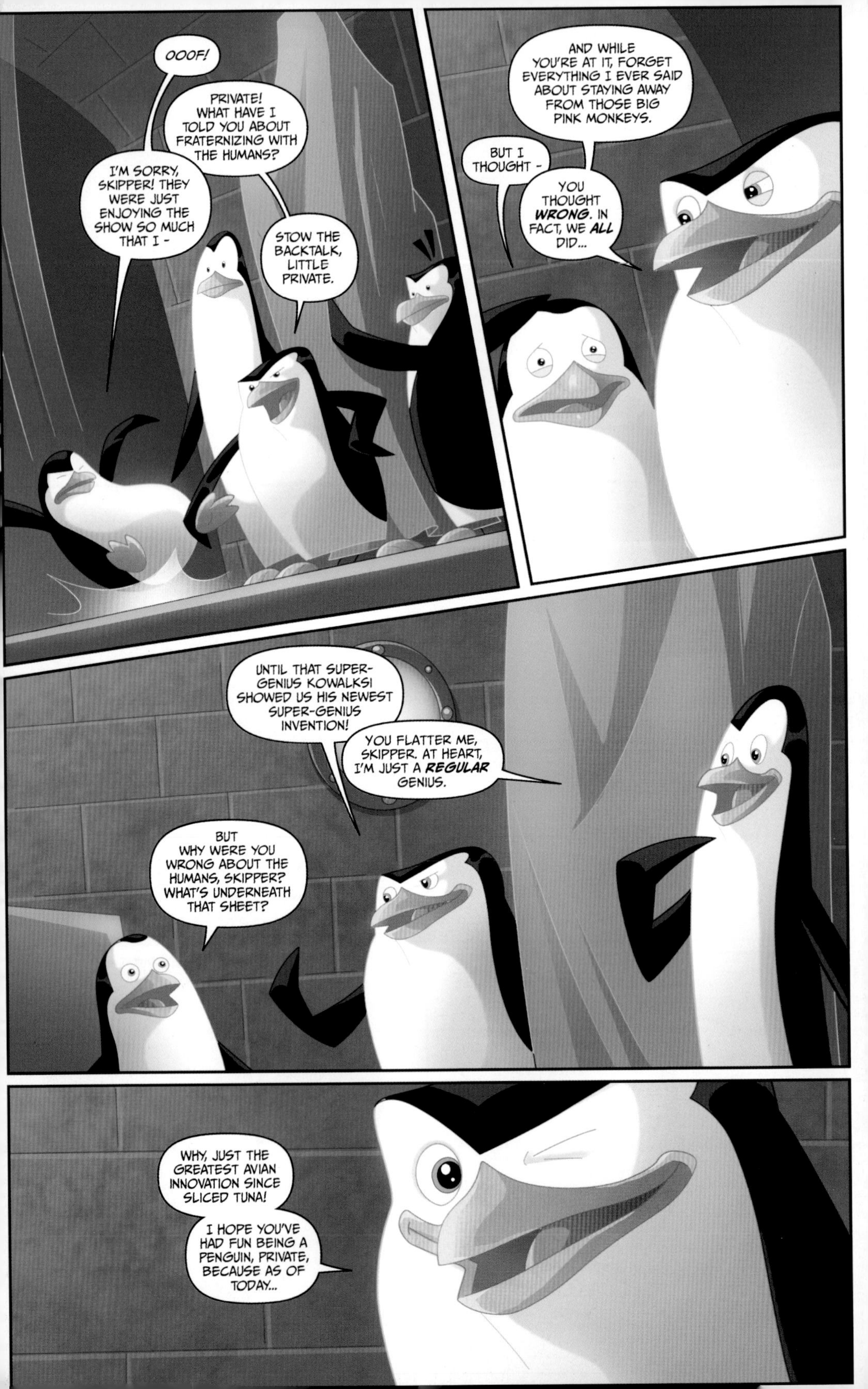
OOOF!
PRIVATE! WHAT HAVE I TOLD YOU ABOUT FRATERNIZING WITH THE HUMANS?
I'M SORRY, SKIPPER! THEY WERE JUST ENJOYING THE SHOW SO MUCH THAT I -
STOW THE BACKTALK, LITTLE PRIVATE.
AND WHILE YOU'RE AT IT, FORGET EVERYTHING I EVER SAID ABOUT STAYING AWAY FROM THOSE BIG PINK MONKEYS.
BUT I THOUGHT -
YOU THOUGHT WRONG. IN FACT, WE ALL DID...
UNTIL THAT SUPER-GENIUS KOWALKSI SHOWED US HIS NEWEST SUPER-GENIUS INVENTION!
YOU FLATTER ME, SKIPPER. AT HEART, I'M JUST A REGULAR GENIUS.
BUT WHY WERE YOU WRONG ABOUT THE HUMANS, SKIPPER? WHAT'S UNDERNEATH THAT SHEET?
WHY, JUST THE GREATEST AVIAN INNOVATION SINCE SLICED TUNA!
I HOPE YOU'VE HAD FUN BEING A PENGUIN, PRIVATE, BECAUSE AS OF TODAY...

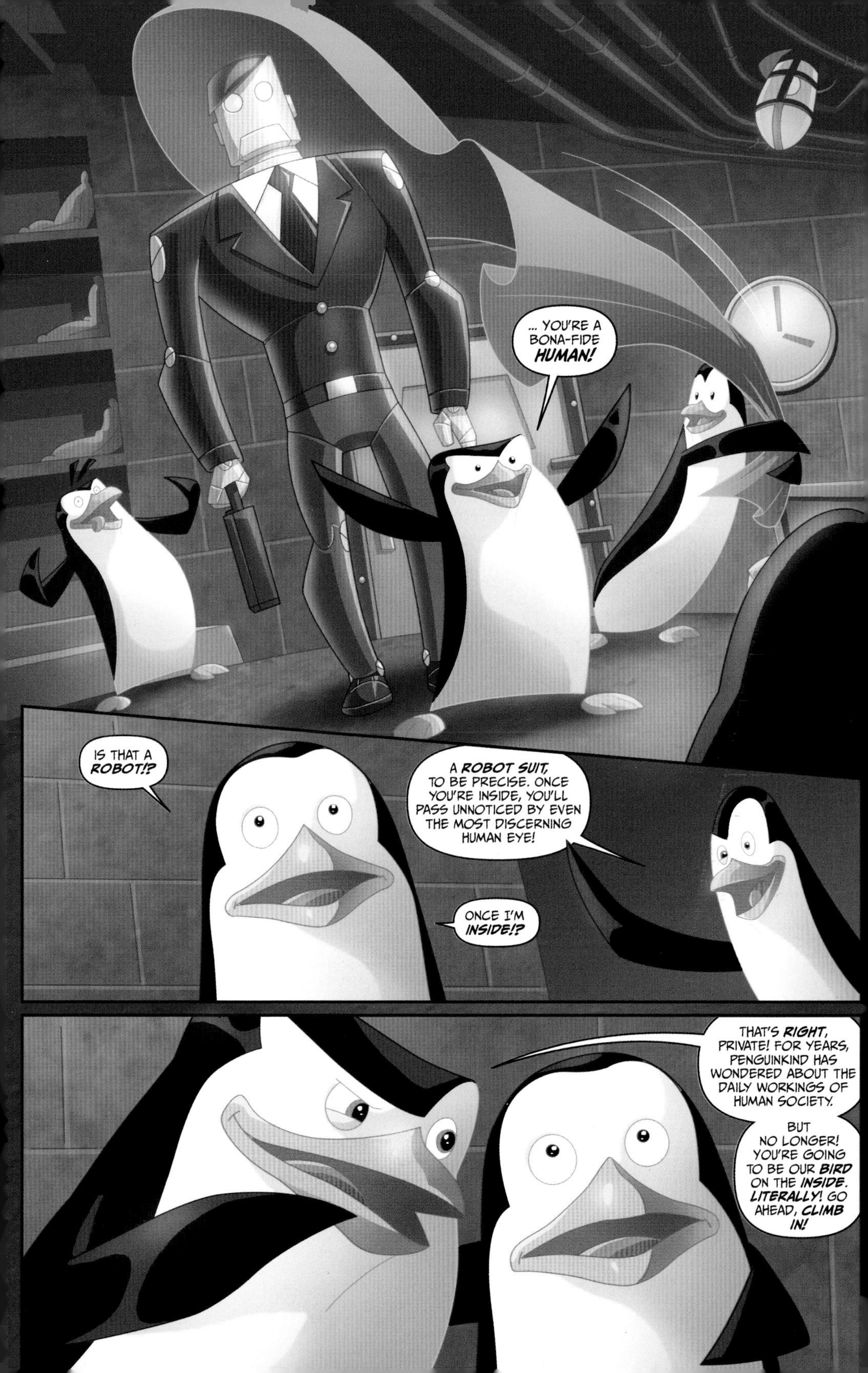
... YOU'RE A BONA-FIDE HUMAN!
IS THAT A ROBOT!?
A ROBOT SUIT, TO BE PRECISE. ONCE YOU'RE INSIDE, YOU'LL PASS UNNOTICED BY EVEN THE MOST DISCERNING HUMAN EYE!
ONCE I'M INSIDE!?
THAT'S RIGHT, PRIVATE! FOR YEARS, PENGUINKIND HAS WONDERED ABOUT THE DAILY WORKINGS OF HUMAN SOCIETY.
BUT NO LONGER! YOU'RE GOING TO BE OUR BIRD ON THE INSIDE. LITERALLY! GO AHEAD, CLIMB IN!

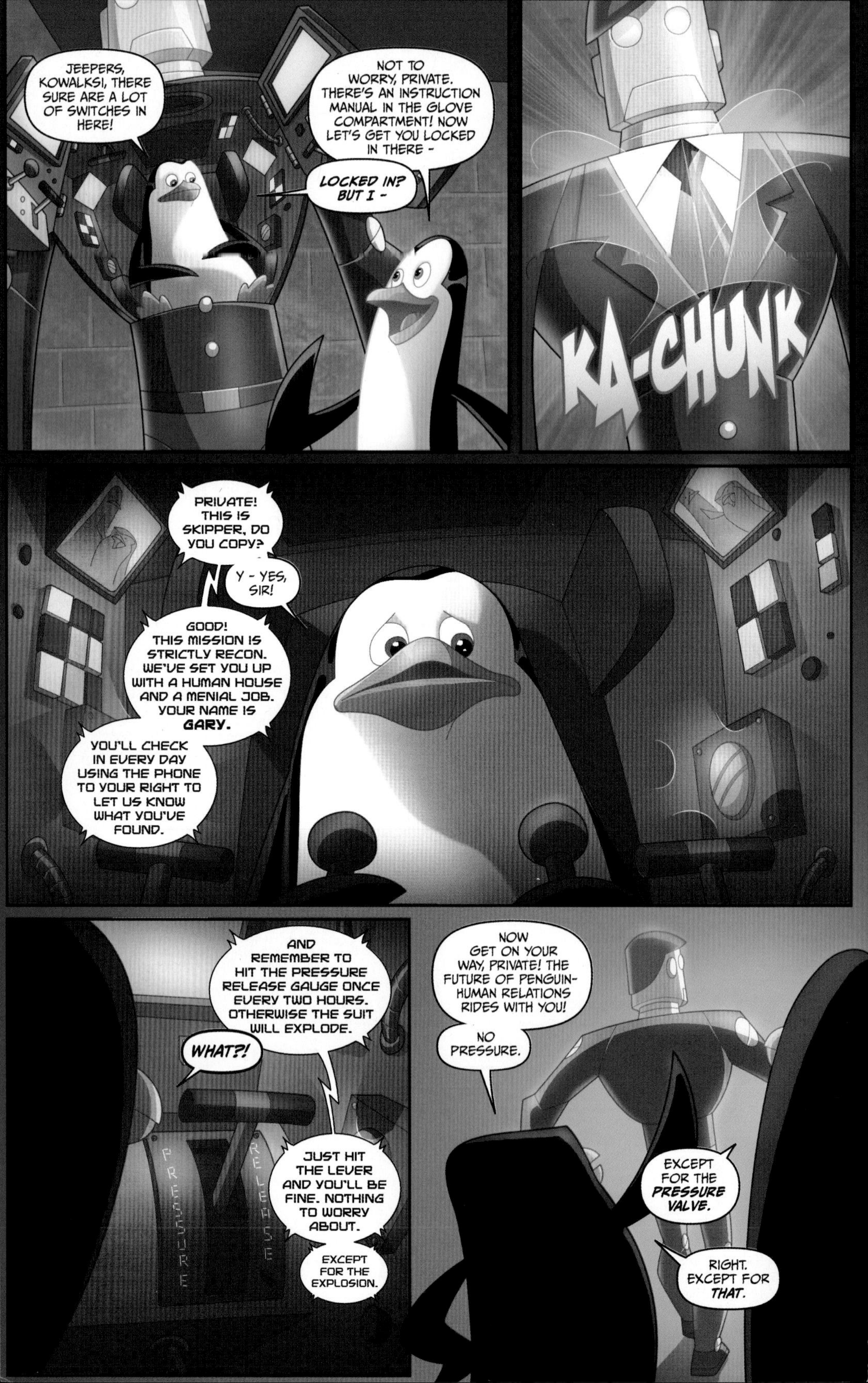

JEEPERS, KOWALKSI, THERE SURE ARE A LOT OF SWITCHES IN HERE!
NOT TO WORRY, PRIVATE. THERE'S AN INSTRUCTION MANUAL IN THE GLOVE COMPARTMENT! NOW LET'S GET YOU LOCKED IN THERE -
LOCKED IN? BUT I -
KA-CHUNK
PRIVATE! THIS IS SKIPPER, DO YOU COPY?
Y - YES, SIR!
GOOD! THIS MISSION IS STRICTLY RECON. WE'VE SET YOU UP WITH A HUMAN HOUSE AND A MENIAL JOB. YOUR NAME IS GARY.
YOU'LL CHECK IN EVERY DAY USING THE PHONE TO YOUR RIGHT TO LET US KNOW WHAT YOU'VE FOUND.
AND REMEMBER TO HIT THE PRESSURE RELEASE GAUGE ONCE EVERY TWO HOURS. OTHERWISE THE SUIT WILL EXPLODE.
WHAT?!
PRESSURE
RELEASE
JUST HIT THE LEVER AND YOU'LL BE FINE. NOTHING TO WORRY ABOUT.
EXCEPT FOR THE EXPLOSION.
NOW GET ON YOUR WAY, PRIVATE! THE FUTURE OF PENGUIN-HUMAN RELATIONS RIDES WITH YOU!
NO PRESSURE.
EXCEPT FOR THE PRESSURE VALVE.
RIGHT. EXCEPT FOR THAT.

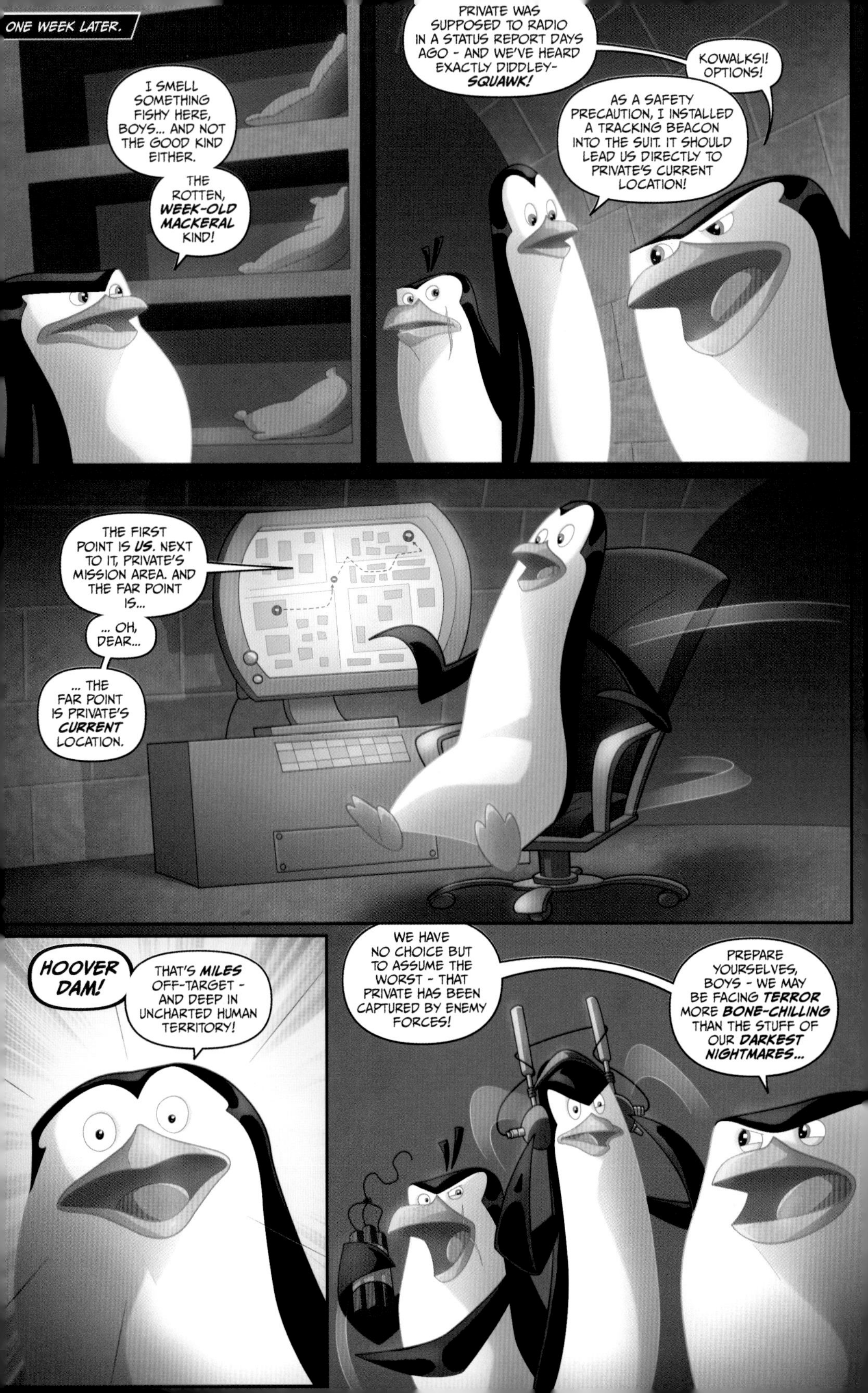
ONE WEEK LATER.
I SMELL SOMETHING FISHY HERE, BOYS... AND NOT THE GOOD KIND EITHER.
THE ROTTEN, WEEK-OLD MACKERAL KIND!
PRIVATE WAS SUPPOSED TO RADIO IN A STATUS REPORT DAYS AGO - AND WE'VE HEARD EXACTLY DIDDLEY-SQUAWK!
KOWALKSI! OPTIONS!
AS A SAFETY PRECAUTION, I INSTALLED A TRACKING BEACON INTO THE SUIT. IT SHOULD LEAD US DIRECTLY TO PRIVATE'S CURRENT LOCATION!
THE FIRST POINT IS US. NEXT TO IT, PRIVATE'S MISSION AREA. AND THE FAR POINT IS...
... OH, DEAR...
... THE FAR POINT IS PRIVATE'S CURRENT LOCATION.
HOOVER DAM!
THAT'S MILES OFF-TARGET - AND DEEP IN UNCHARTED HUMAN TERRITORY!
WE HAVE NO CHOICE BUT TO ASSUME THE WORST - THAT PRIVATE HAS BEEN CAPTURED BY ENEMY FORCES!
PREPARE YOURSELVES, BOYS - WE MAY BE FACING TERROR MORE BONE-CHILLING THAN THE STUFF OF OUR DARKEST NIGHTMARES...

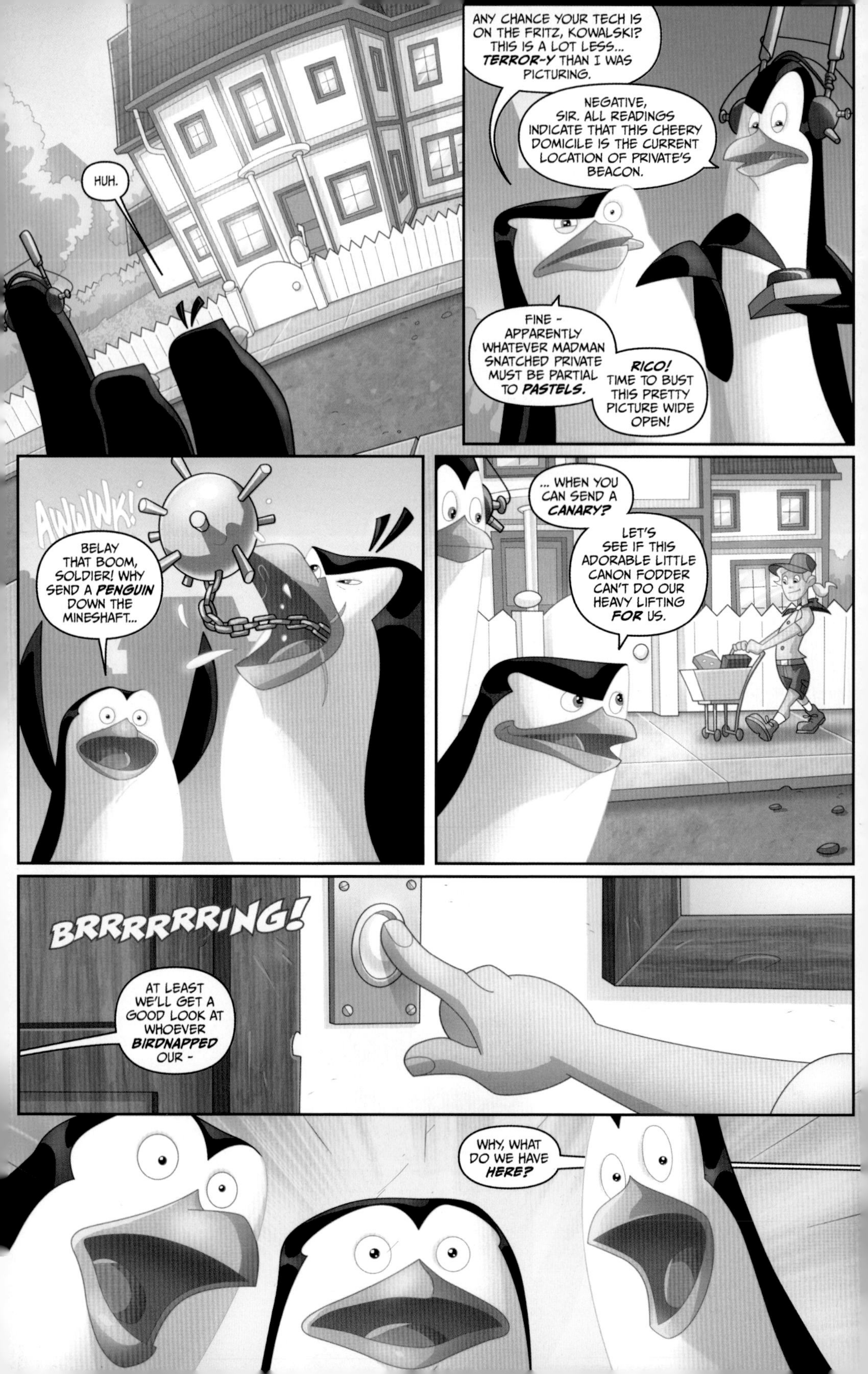
HUH.
ANY CHANCE YOUR TECH IS ON THE FRITZ, KOWALSKI? THIS IS A LOT LESS... TERROR-Y THAN I WAS PICTURING.
NEGATIVE, SIR. ALL READINGS INDICATE THAT THIS CHEERY DOMICILE IS THE CURRENT LOCATION OF PRIVATE'S BEACON.
FINE - APPARENTLY WHATEVER MADMAN SNATCHED PRIVATE MUST BE PARTIAL TO PASTELS.
RICO! TIME TO BUST THIS PRETTY PICTURE WIDE OPEN!
AWWWK!
BELAY THAT BOOM, SOLDIER! WHY SEND A PENGUIN DOWN THE MINESHAFT...
... WHEN YOU CAN SEND A CANARY?
LET'S SEE IF THIS ADORABLE LITTLE CANON FODDER CAN'T DO OUR HEAVY LIFTING FOR US.
BRRRRRRING!
AT LEAST WE'LL GET A GOOD LOOK AT WHOEVER BIRDNAPPED OUR -
WHY, WHAT DO WE HAVE HERE?

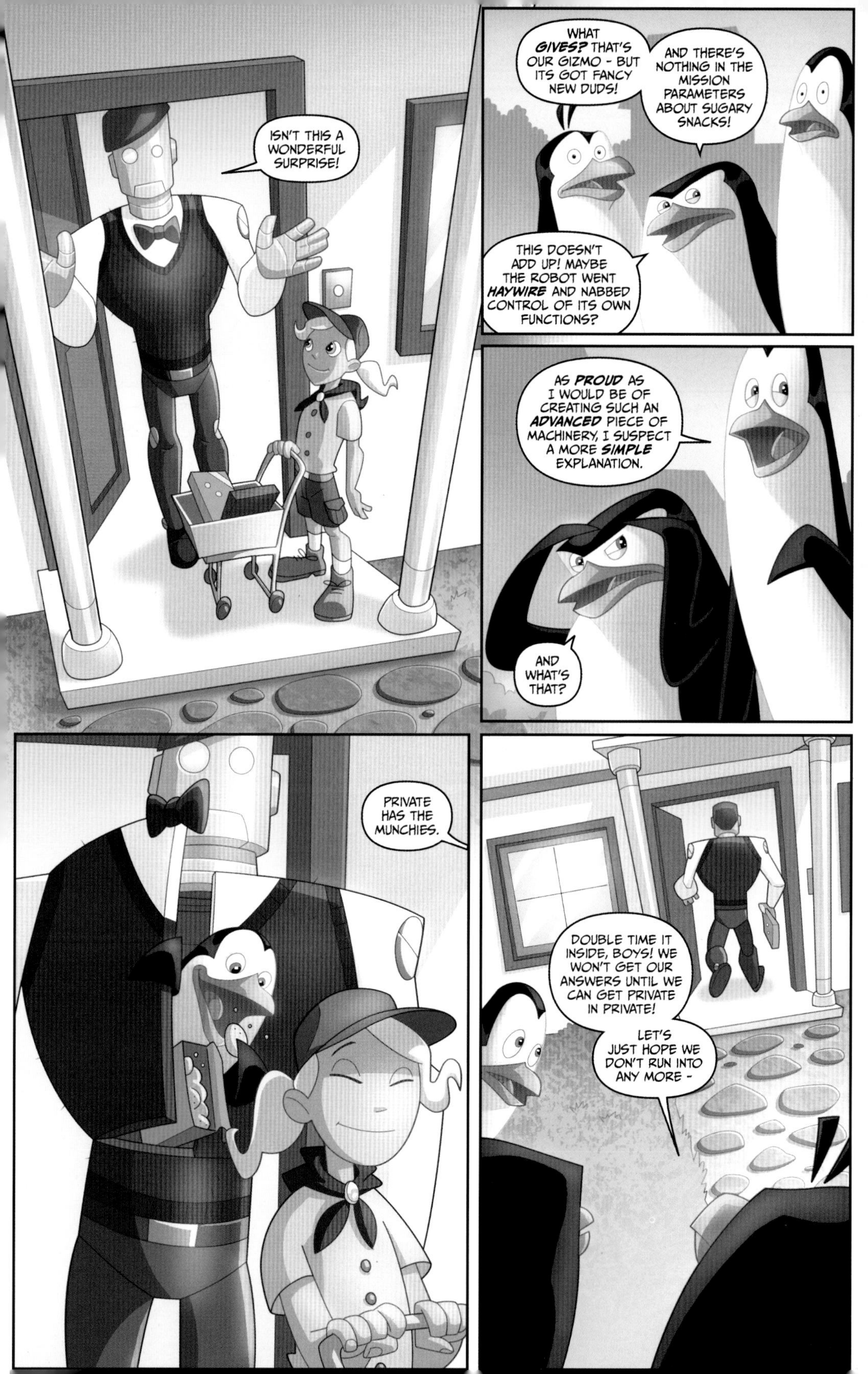
ISN'T THIS A WONDERFUL SURPRISE!
WHAT GIVES? THAT'S OUR GIZMO - BUT ITS GOT FANCY NEW DUDS!
AND THERE'S NOTHING IN THE MISSION PARAMETERS ABOUT SUGARY SNACKS!
THIS DOESN'T ADD UP! MAYBE THE ROBOT WENT HAYWIRE AND NABBED CONTROL OF ITS OWN FUNCTIONS?
AS PROUD AS I WOULD BE OF CREATING SUCH AN ADVANCED PIECE OF MACHINERY, I SUSPECT A MORE SIMPLE EXPLANATION.
AND WHAT'S THAT?
PRIVATE HAS THE MUNCHIES.
DOUBLE TIME IT INSIDE, BOYS! WE WON'T GET OUR ANSWERS UNTIL WE CAN GET PRIVATE IN PRIVATE!
LET'S JUST HOPE WE DON'T RUN INTO ANY MORE -

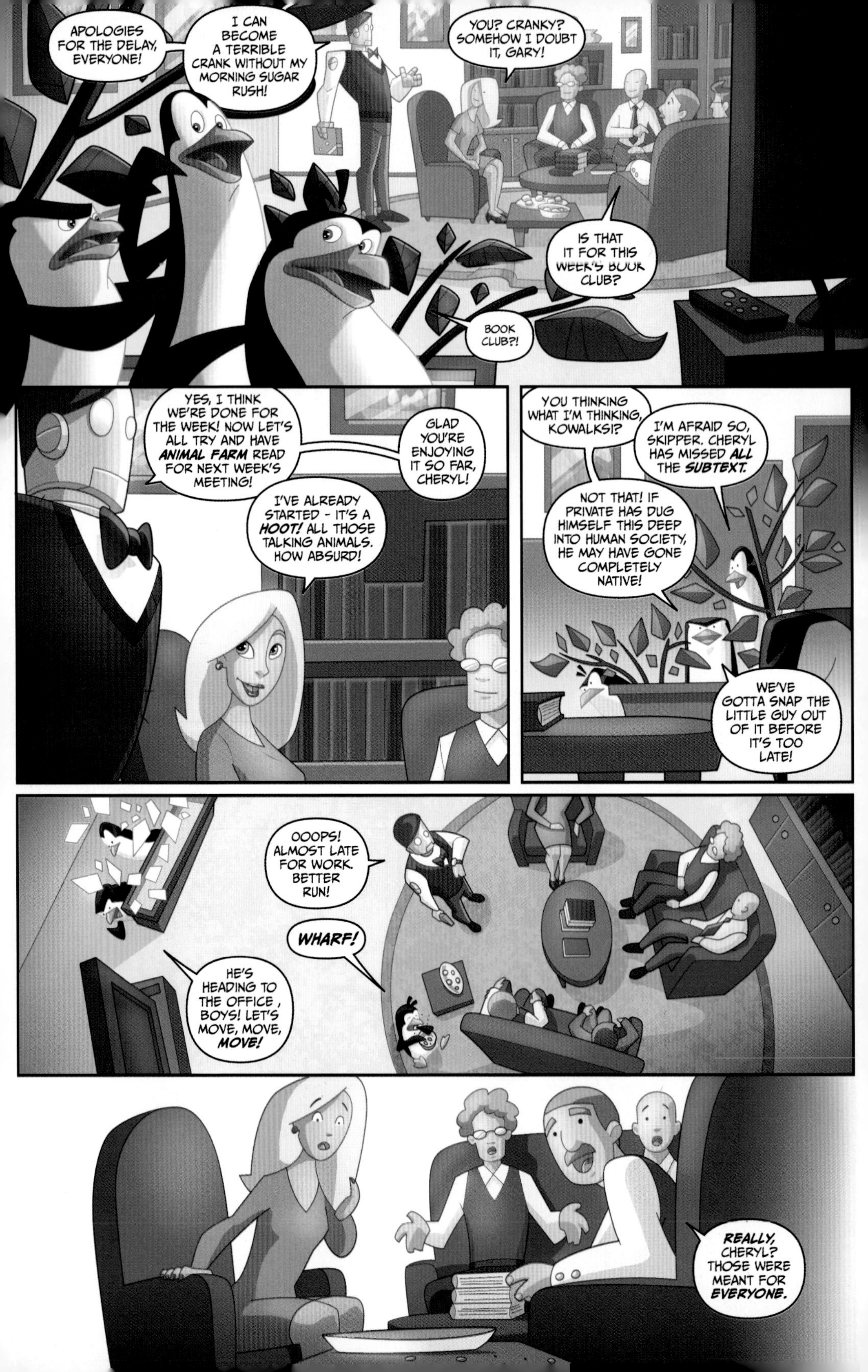
APOLOGIES FOR THE DELAY, EVERYONE!
I CAN BECOME A TERRIBLE CRANK WITHOUT MY MORNING SUGAR RUSH!
YOU? CRANKY? SOMEHOW I DOUBT IT, GARY!
IS THAT IT FOR THIS WEEK'S BOOK CLUB?
BOOK CLUB?!
YES, I THINK WE'RE DONE FOR THE WEEK! NOW LET'S ALL TRY AND HAVE ANIMAL FARM READ FOR NEXT WEEK'S MEETING!
I'VE ALREADY STARTED - IT'S A HOOT! ALL THOSE TALKING ANIMALS. HOW ABSURD!
GLAD YOU'RE ENJOYING IT SO FAR, CHERYL!
YOU THINKING WHAT I'M THINKING, KOWALKSI?
I'M AFRAID SO, SKIPPER. CHERYL HAS MISSED ALL THE SUBTEXT.
NOT THAT! IF PRIVATE HAS DUG HIMSELF THIS DEEP INTO HUMAN SOCIETY, HE MAY HAVE GONE COMPLETELY NATIVE!
WE'VE GOTTA SNAP THE LITTLE GUY OUT OF IT BEFORE IT'S TOO LATE!
OOOPS! ALMOST LATE FOR WORK. BETTER RUN!
WHARF!
HE'S HEADING TO THE OFFICE , BOYS! LET'S MOVE, MOVE, MOVE!
REALLY, CHERYL? THOSE WERE MEANT FOR EVERYONE.

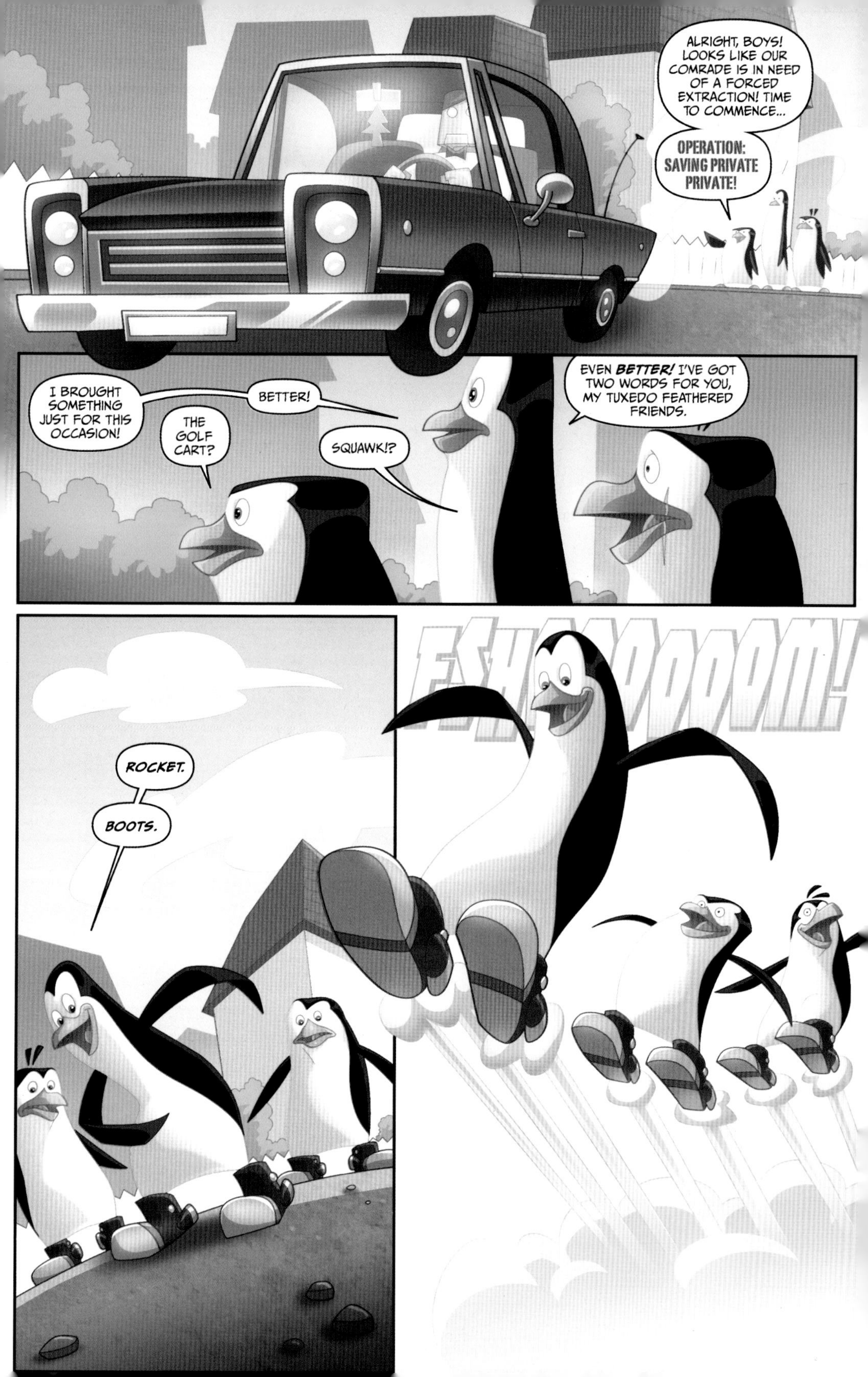
ALRIGHT, BOYS! LOOKS LIKE OUR COMRADE IS IN NEED OF A FORCED EXTRACTION! TIME TO COMMENCE...
OPERATION: SAVING PRIVATE PRIVATE!
I BROUGHT SOMETHING JUST FOR THIS OCCASION!
THE GOLF CART?
BETTER!
SQUAWK!?
EVEN BETTER! I'VE GOT TWO WORDS FOR YOU, MY TUXEDO FEATHERED FRIENDS.
ROCKET.
BOOTS.
FSHOOOOOOM!

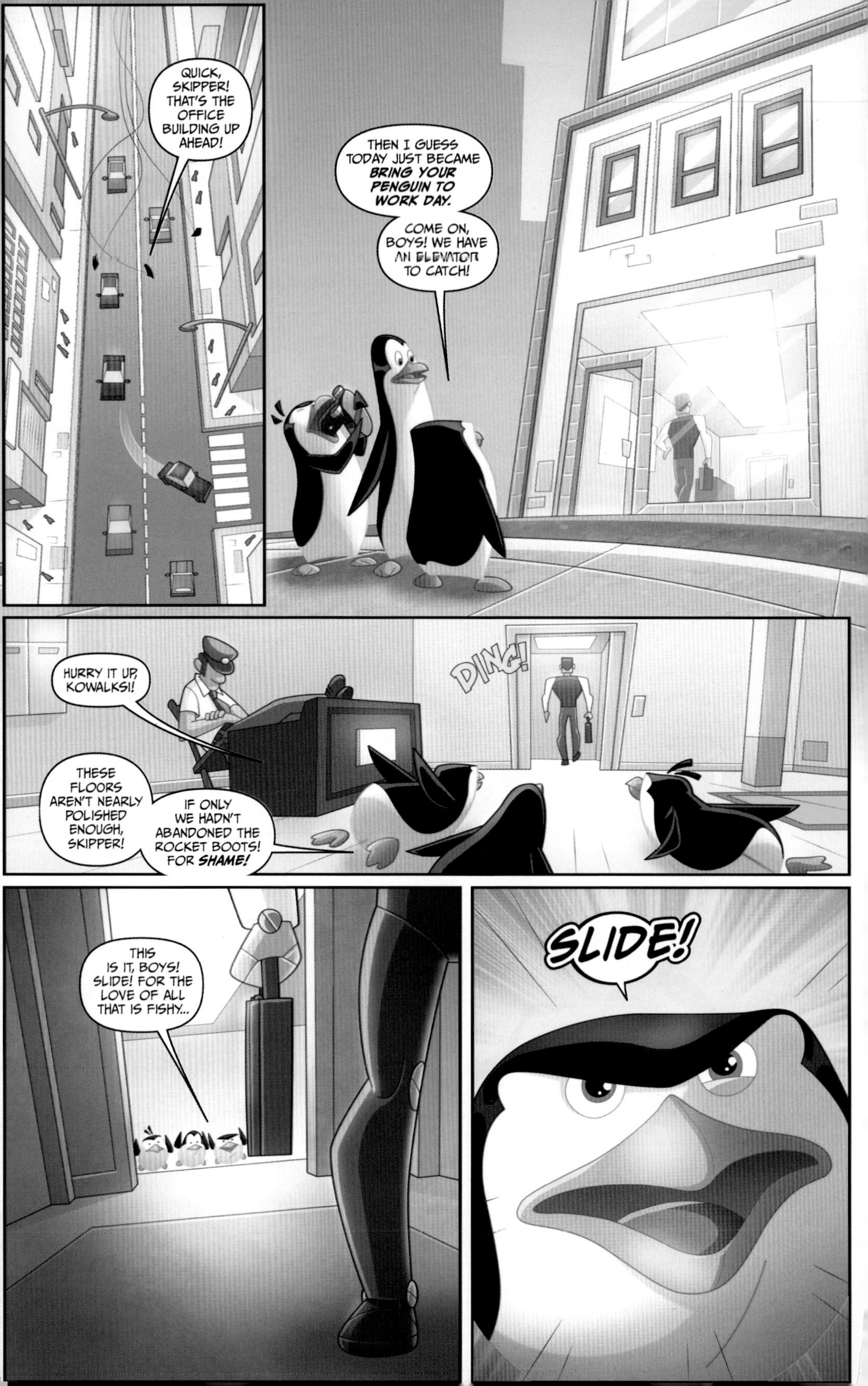
QUICK, SKIPPER! THAT'S THE OFFICE BUILDING UP AHEAD!
THEN I GUESS TODAY JUST BECAME BRING YOUR PENGUIN TO WORK DAY.
COME ON, BOYS! WE HAVE AN ELEVATOR TO CATCH!
DING!
HURRY IT UP, KOWALKSI!
THESE FLOORS AREN'T NEARLY POLISHED ENOUGH, SKIPPER!
IF ONLY WE HADN'T ABANDONED THE ROCKET BOOTS! FOR SHAME!
THIS IS IT, BOYS! SLIDE! FOR THE LOVE OF ALL THAT IS FISHY...
SLIDE!

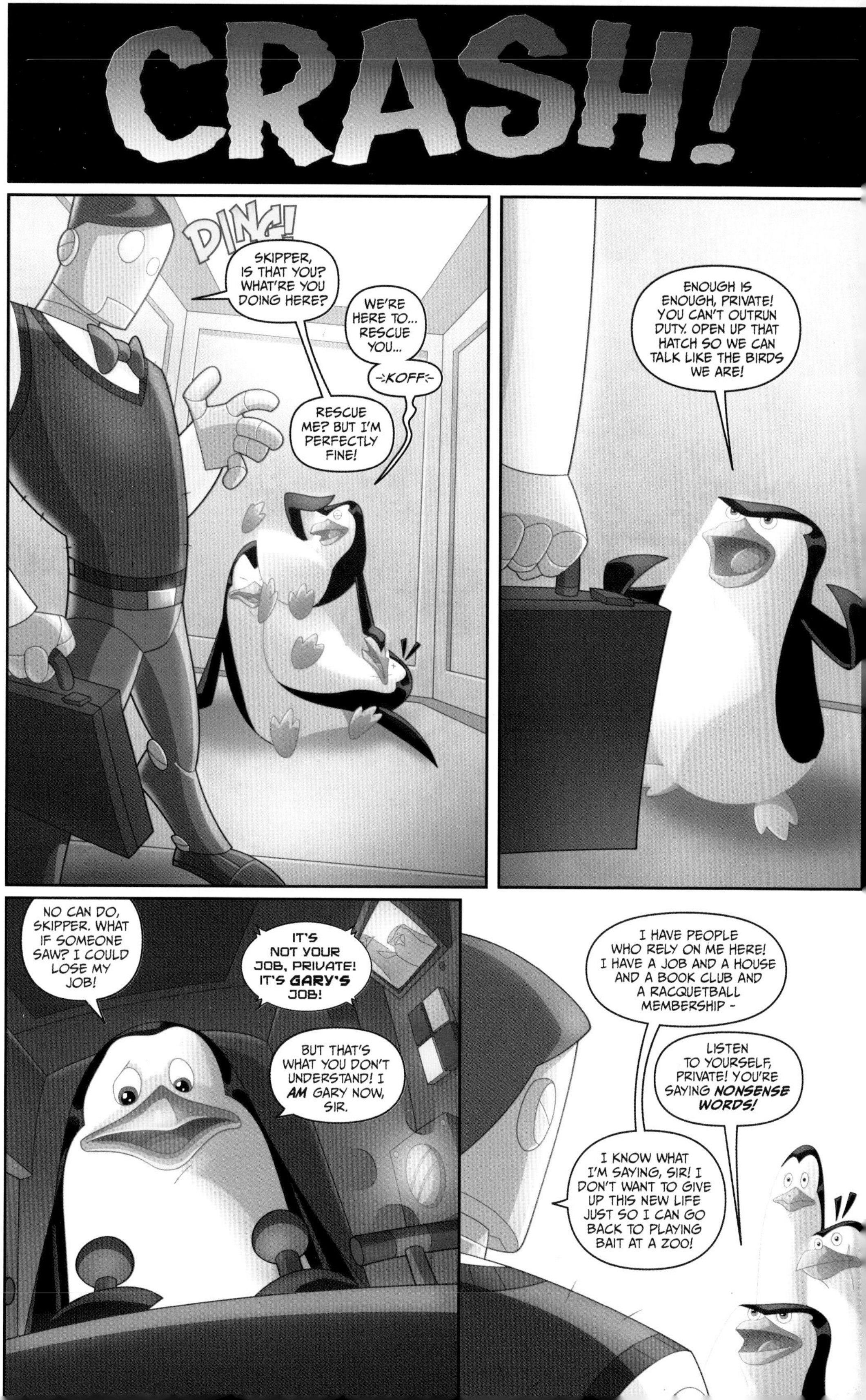
CRASH!
DING!
SKIPPER, IS THAT YOU? WHAT'RE YOU DOING HERE?
WE'RE HERE TO... RESCUE YOU...
-KOFF-
RESCUE ME? BUT I'M PERFECTLY FINE!
ENOUGH IS ENOUGH, PRIVATE! YOU CAN'T OUTRUN DUTY. OPEN UP THAT HATCH SO WE CAN TALK LIKE THE BIRDS WE ARE!
NO CAN DO, SKIPPER. WHAT IF SOMEONE SAW? I COULD LOSE MY JOB!
IT'S NOT YOUR JOB, PRIVATE! IT'S GARY'S JOB!
BUT THAT'S WHAT YOU DON'T UNDERSTAND! I AM GARY NOW, SIR.
I HAVE PEOPLE WHO RELY ON ME HERE! I HAVE A JOB AND A HOUSE AND A BOOK CLUB AND A RACQUETBALL MEMBERSHIP -
LISTEN TO YOURSELF, PRIVATE! YOU'RE SAYING NONSENSE WORDS!
I KNOW WHAT I'M SAYING, SIR! I DON'T WANT TO GIVE UP THIS NEW LIFE JUST SO I CAN GO BACK TO PLAYING BAIT AT A ZOO!

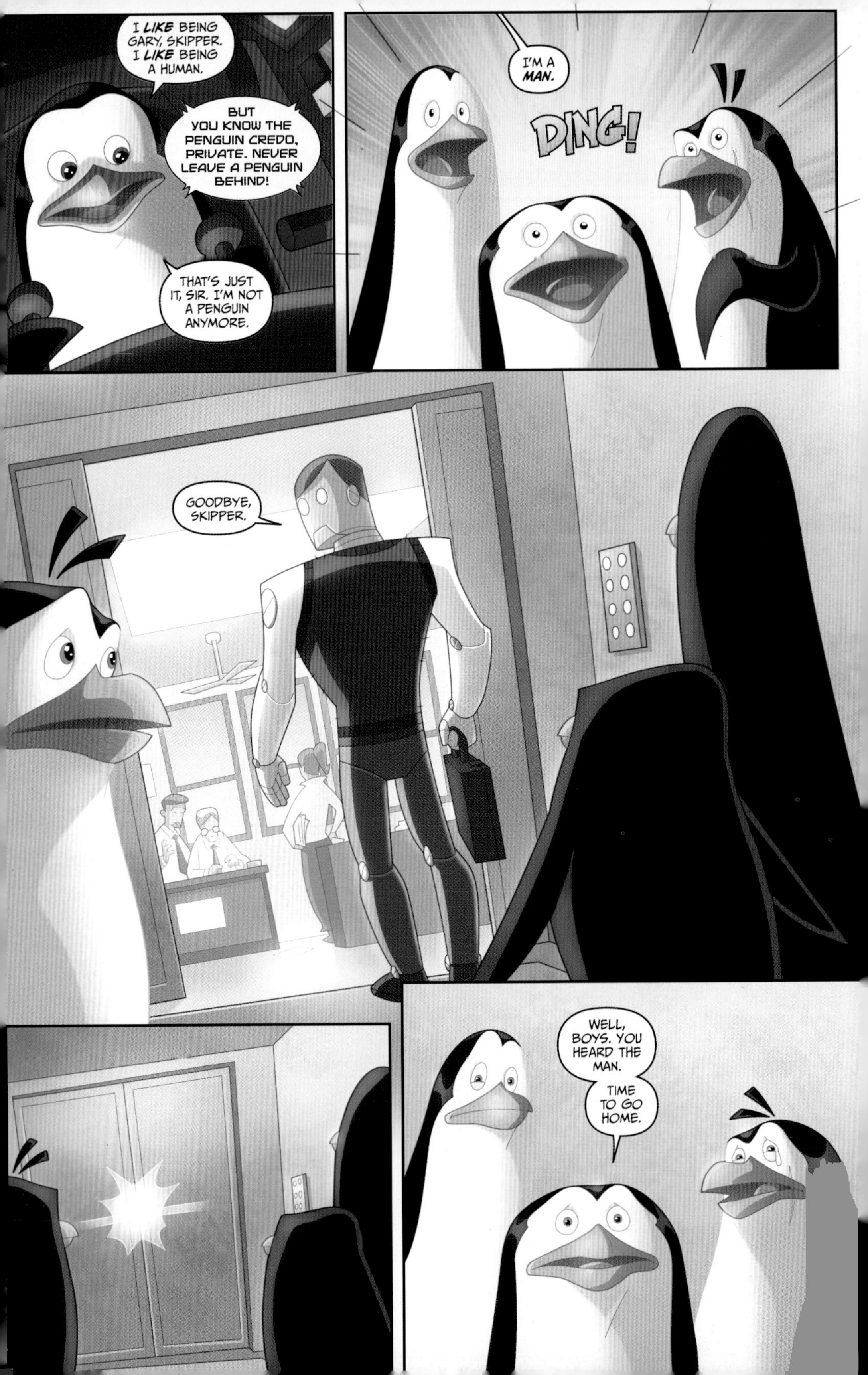

I LIKE BEING GARY, SKIPPER. I LIKE BEING A HUMAN.
BUT YOU KNOW THE PENGUIN CREDO, PRIVATE. NEVER LEAVE A PENGUIN BEHIND!
THAT'S JUST IT, SIR. I'M NOT A PENGUIN ANYMORE.
I'M A MAN.
DING!
GOODBYE, SKIPPER.
WELL, BOYS. YOU HEARD THE MAN.
TIME TO GO HOME.

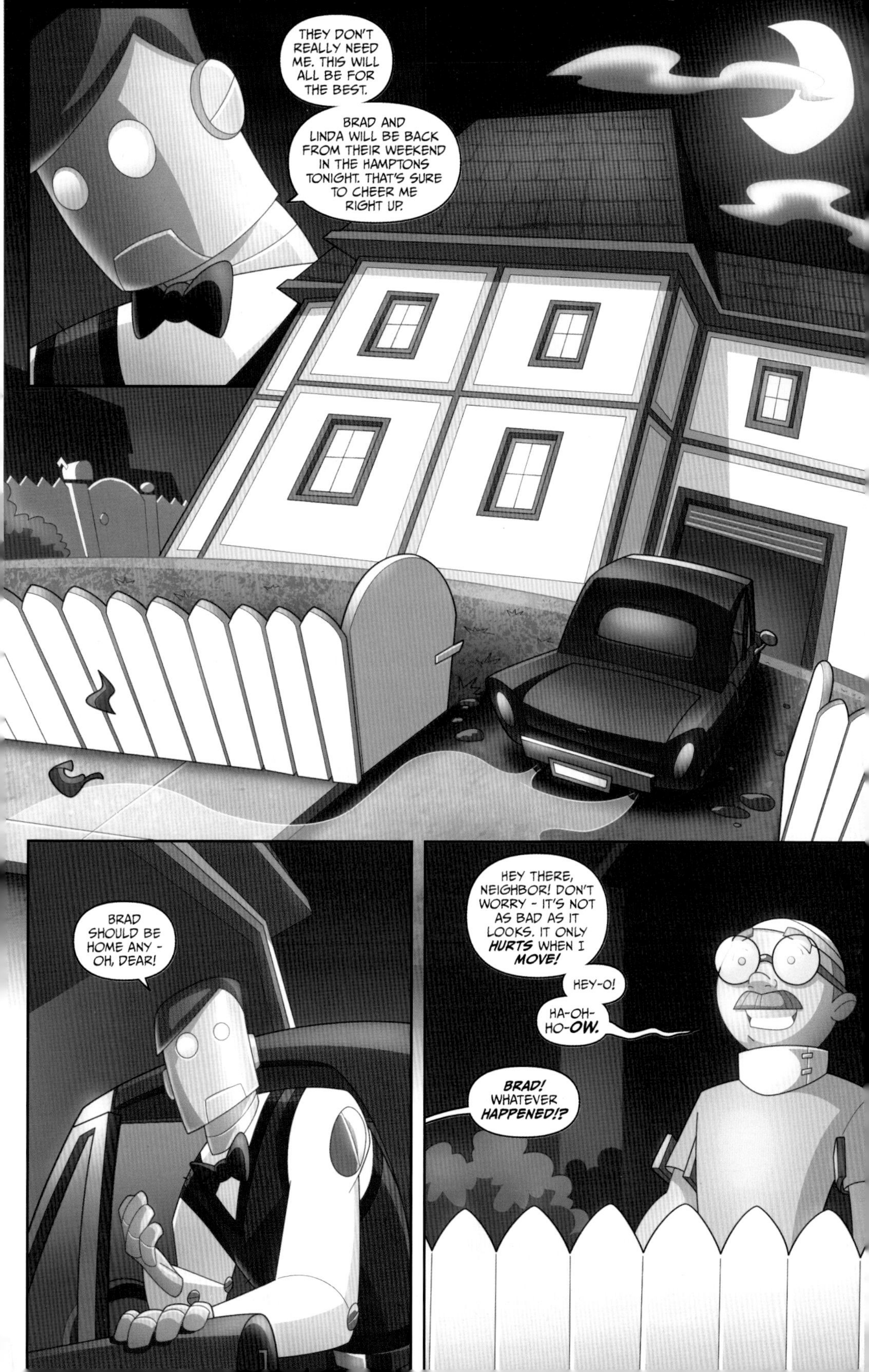
THEY DON'T REALLY NEED ME. THIS WILL ALL BE FOR THE BEST.
BRAD AND LINDA WILL BE BACK FROM THEIR WEEKEND IN THE HAMPTONS TONIGHT. THAT'S SURE TO CHEER ME RIGHT UP.
BRAD SHOULD BE HOME ANY - OH, DEAR!
HEY THERE, NEIGHBOR! DON'T WORRY - IT'S NOT AS BAD AS IT LOOKS. IT ONLY HURTS WHEN I MOVE!
HEY-O!
HA-OH-HO-OW.
BRAD! WHATEVER HAPPENED!?

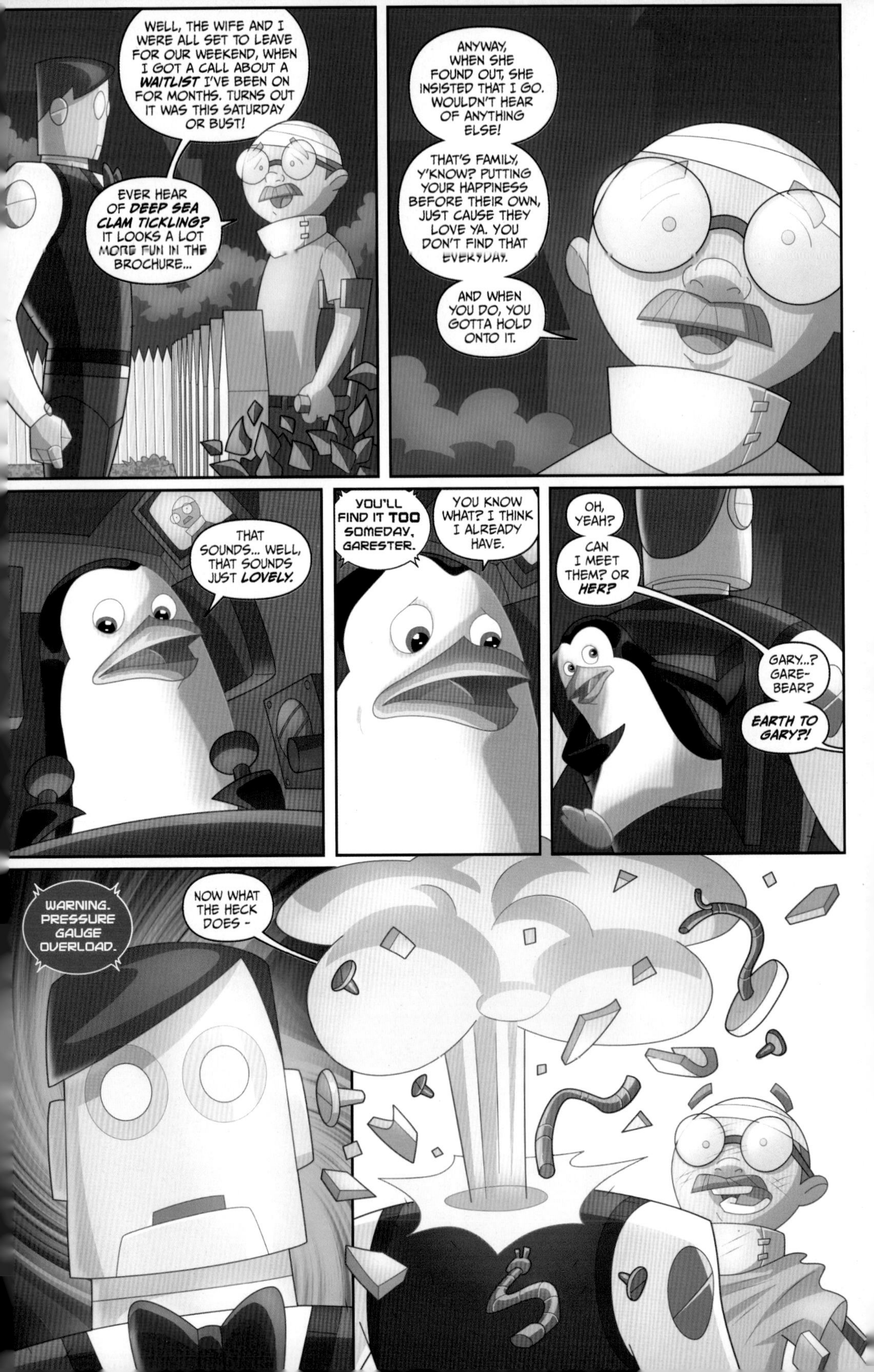
WELL, THE WIFE AND I WERE ALL SET TO LEAVE FOR OUR WEEKEND, WHEN I GOT A CALL ABOUT A WAITLIST I'VE BEEN ON FOR MONTHS. TURNS OUT IT WAS THIS SATURDAY OR BUST!
EVER HEAR OF DEEP SEA CLAM TICKLING? IT LOOKS A LOT MORE FUN IN THE BROCHURE...
ANYWAY, WHEN SHE FOUND OUT, SHE INSISTED THAT I GO. WOULDN'T HEAR OF ANYTHING ELSE!
THAT'S FAMILY, Y'KNOW? PUTTING YOUR HAPPINESS BEFORE THEIR OWN, JUST CAUSE THEY LOVE YA. YOU DON'T FIND THAT EVERYDAY.
AND WHEN YOU DO, YOU GOTTA HOLD ONTO IT.
THAT SOUNDS... WELL, THAT SOUNDS JUST LOVELY.
YOU'LL FIND IT TOO SOMEDAY, GARESTER.
YOU KNOW WHAT? I THINK I ALREADY HAVE.
OH, YEAH?
CAN I MEET THEM? OR HER?
GARY...? GARE-BEAR?
EARTH TO GARY?!
WARNING. PRESSURE GAUGE OVERLOAD.
NOW WHAT THE HECK DOES -

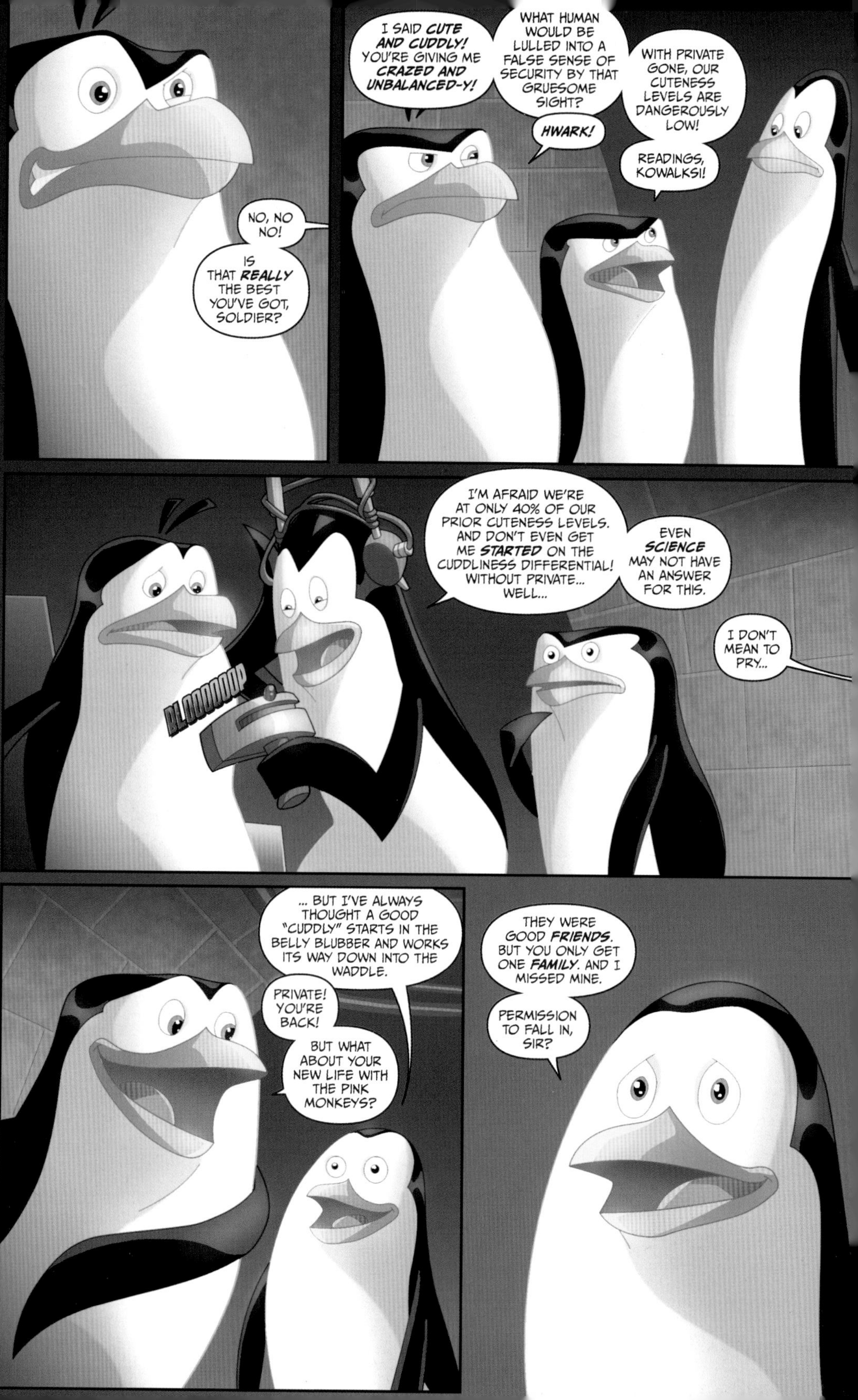
NO, NO NO!
IS THAT REALLY THE BEST YOU'VE GOT, SOLDIER?
I SAID CUTE AND CUDDLY! YOU'RE GIVING ME CRAZED AND UNBALANCED-Y!
WHAT HUMAN WOULD BE LULLED INTO A FALSE SENSE OF SECURITY BY THAT GRUESOME SIGHT?
HWARK!
WITH PRIVATE GONE, OUR CUTENESS LEVELS ARE DANGEROUSLY LOW!
READINGS, KOWALKSI!
I'M AFRAID WE'RE AT ONLY 40% OF OUR PRIOR CUTENESS LEVELS. AND DON'T EVEN GET ME STARTED ON THE CUDDLINESS DIFFERENTIAL! WITHOUT PRIVATE... WELL...
BLOOOOOP
EVEN SCIENCE MAY NOT HAVE AN ANSWER FOR THIS.
I DON'T MEAN TO PRY...
... BUT I'VE ALWAYS THOUGHT A GOOD "CUDDLY" STARTS IN THE BELLY BLUBBER AND WORKS ITS WAY DOWN INTO THE WADDLE.
PRIVATE! YOU'RE BACK!
BUT WHAT ABOUT YOUR NEW LIFE WITH THE PINK MONKEYS?
THEY WERE GOOD FRIENDS. BUT YOU ONLY GET ONE FAMILY. AND I MISSED MINE.
PERMISSION TO FALL IN, SIR?

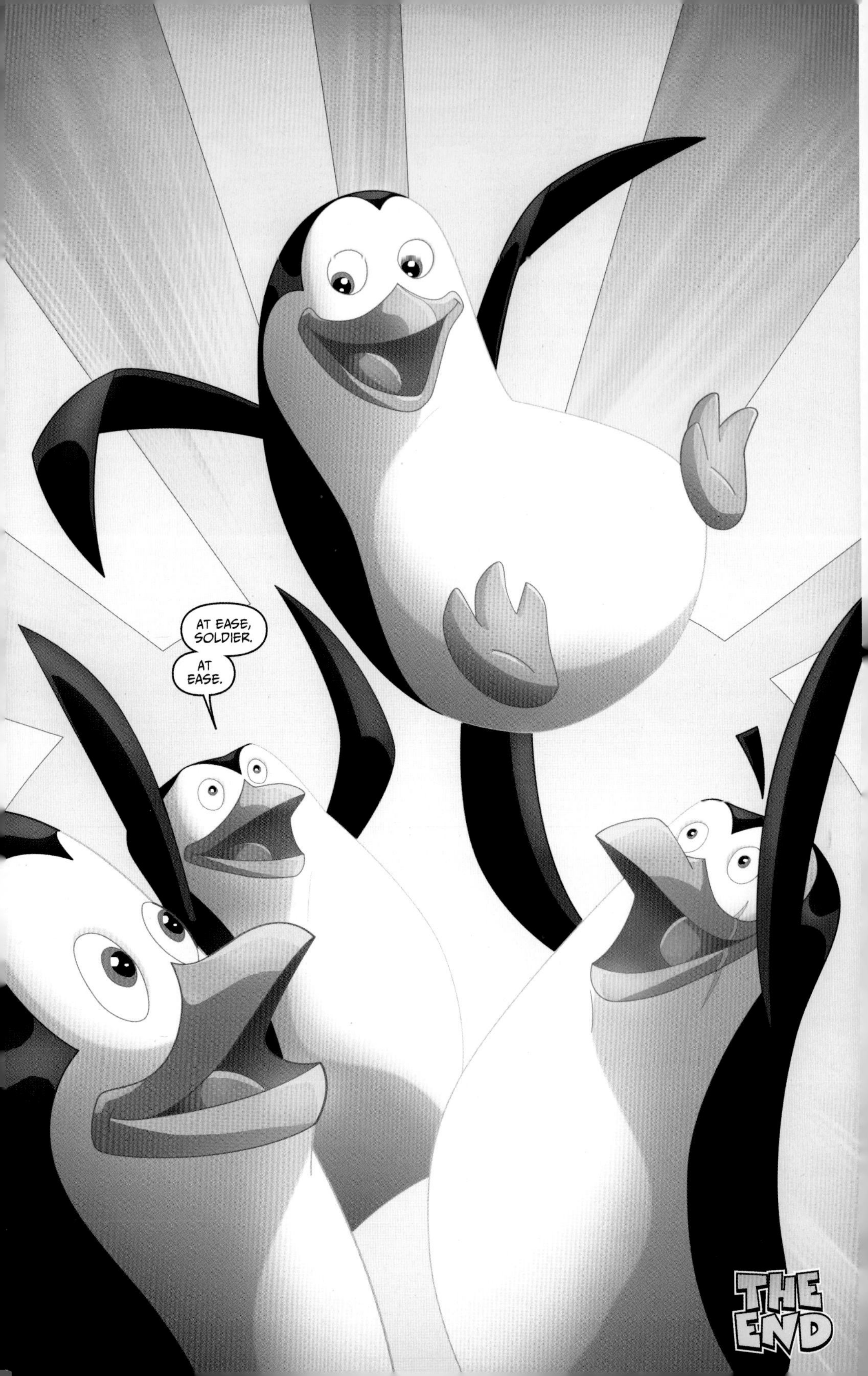
AT EASE, SOLDIER.
AT EASE.
THE END

Subway
SHENANIGANS

Written by David Server
and Jackson Lanzing
Art by James Silvani
Colors by Diego Rodriguez
Letters by Deron Bennett
Edited by Aaron Sparrow

MISSION ACCOMPLISHED, BOYS!

HOORAY!

HIP *HIP*, PRIVATE. THAT'LL TEACH DOCTOR BLOWHOLE NOT TO TINKER WITH THE WORLD SEAFOOD MARKETS.

I'LL GET YOU, PENGEWINS! IF IT'S THE *LAST THING I*

TELL IT TO THE *FEDS.*

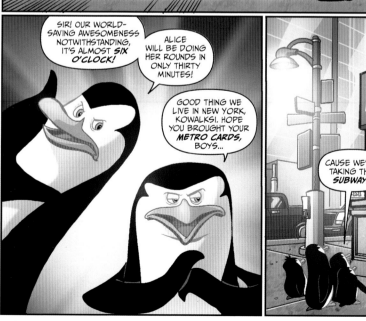

SIR! OUR WORLD-SAVING AWESOMENESS NOTWITHSTANDING, IT'S ALMOST *SIX* O'CLOCK!

ALICE WILL BE DOING HER ROUNDS IN ONLY THIRTY MINUTES!

GOOD THING WE LIVE IN NEW YORK, KOWALSKI! HOPE YOU BROUGHT YOUR *METRO CARDS,* BOYS...

All Trains ↓

CAUSE WE'RE TAKING THE *SUBWAY!*

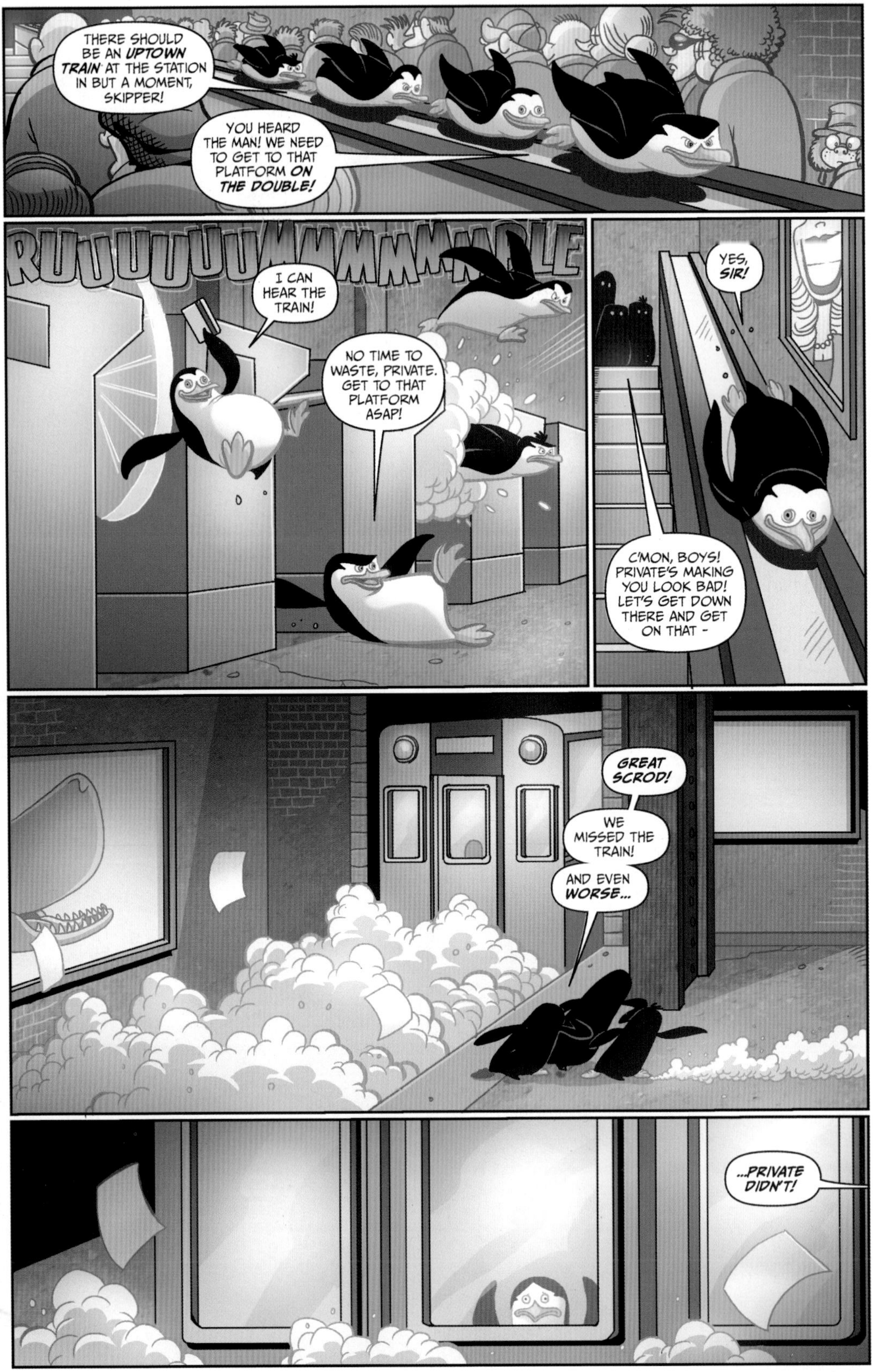
THERE SHOULD BE AN UPTOWN TRAIN AT THE STATION IN BUT A MOMENT, SKIPPER!
YOU HEARD THE MAN! WE NEED TO GET TO THAT PLATFORM ON THE DOUBLE!
RUUUUUUUMMMMMMBLE
I CAN HEAR THE TRAIN!
NO TIME TO WASTE, PRIVATE. GET TO THAT PLATFORM ASAP!
YES, SIR!
C'MON, BOYS! PRIVATE'S MAKING YOU LOOK BAD! LET'S GET DOWN THERE AND GET ON THAT -
GREAT SCROD!
WE MISSED THE TRAIN!
AND EVEN WORSE...
...PRIVATE DIDN'T!

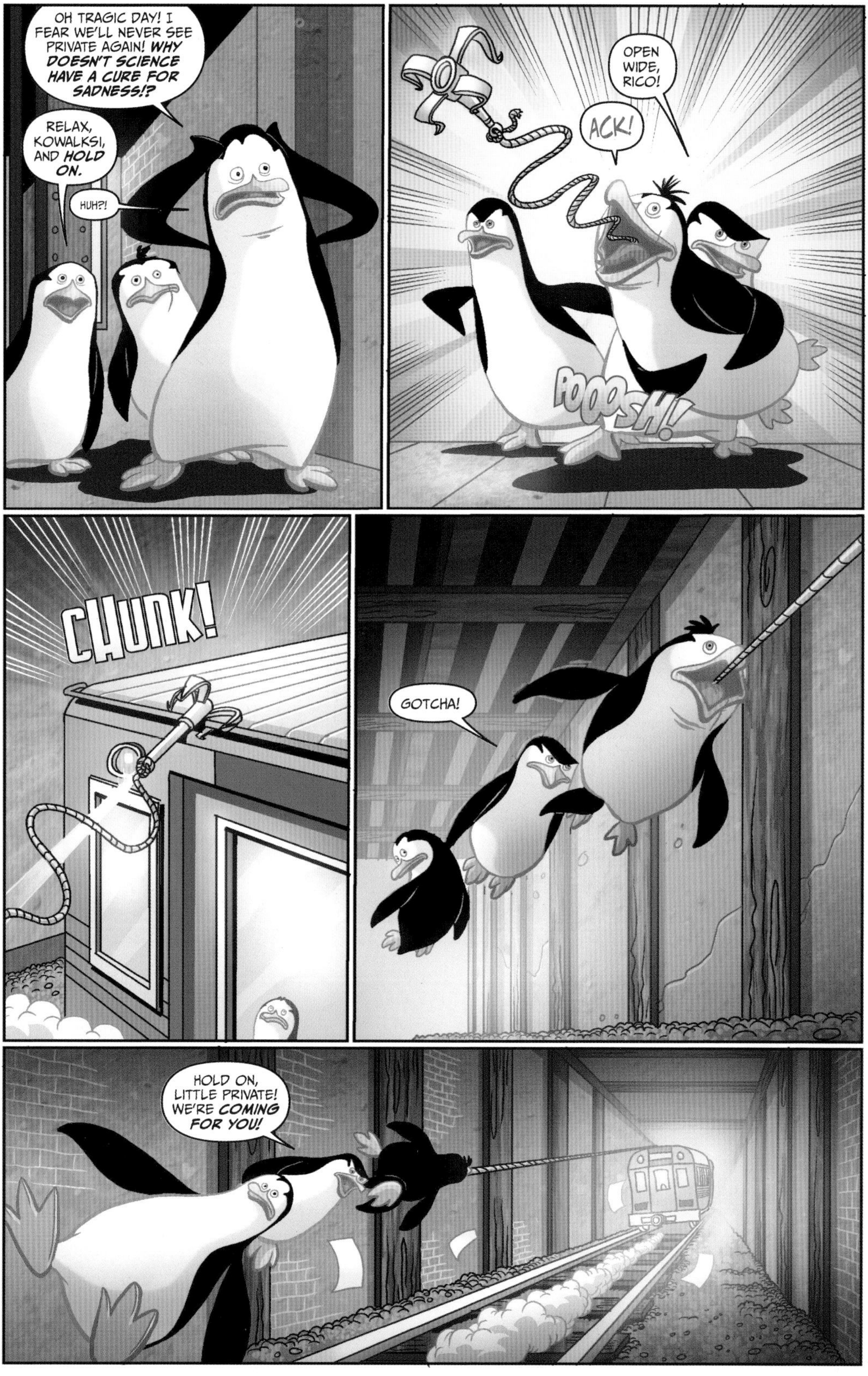
OH TRAGIC DAY! I FEAR WE'LL NEVER SEE PRIVATE AGAIN! WHY DOESN'T SCIENCE HAVE A CURE FOR SADNESS!?
RELAX, KOWALKSI, AND HOLD ON.
HUH?!
OPEN WIDE, RICO!
ACK!
POOOSH!
CHUNK!
GOTCHA!
HOLD ON, LITTLE PRIVATE! WE'RE COMING FOR YOU!

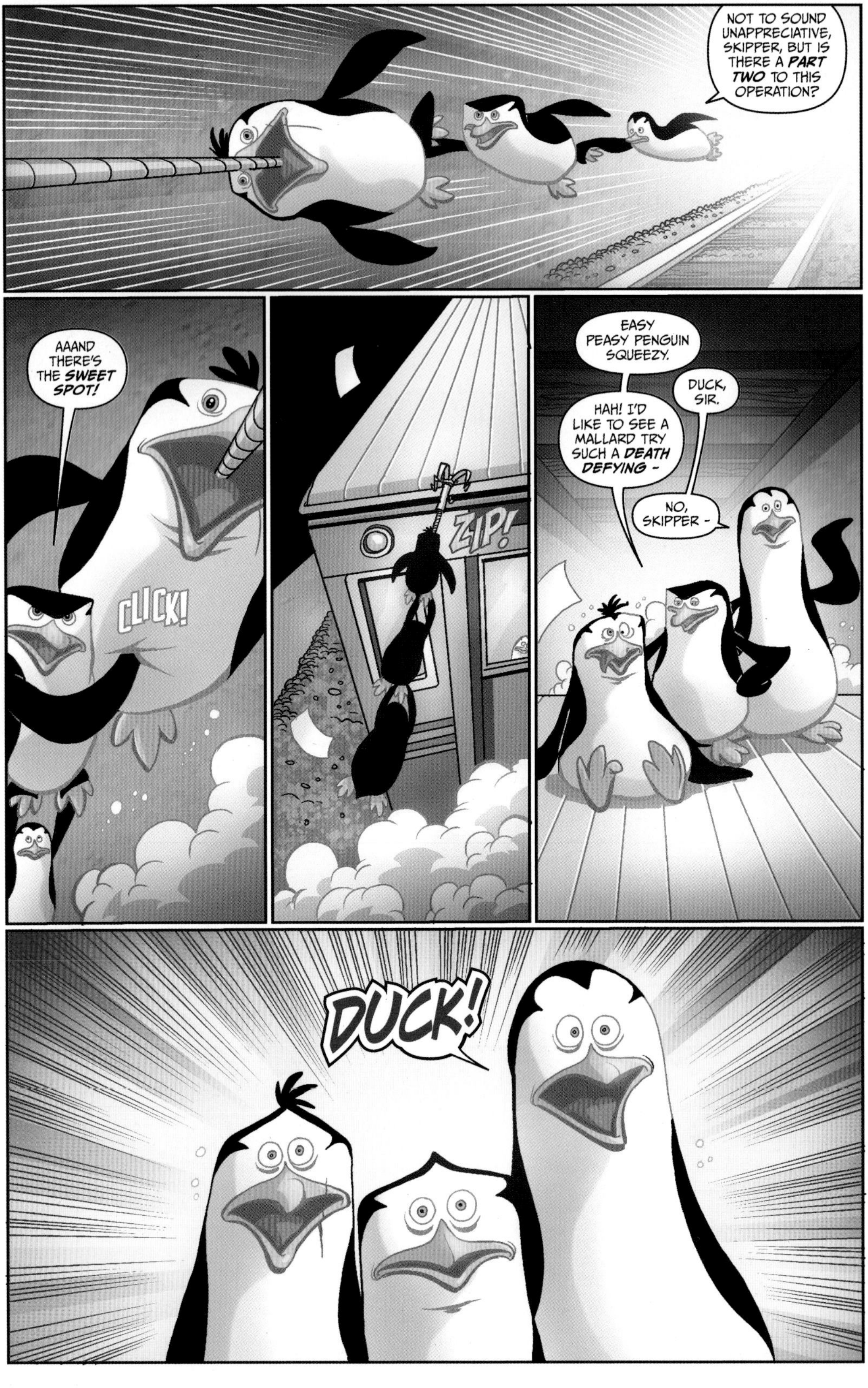
NOT TO SOUND UNAPPRECIATIVE, SKIPPER, BUT IS THERE A **PART TWO** TO THIS OPERATION?
AAAND THERE'S THE **SWEET SPOT!**
CLICK!
ZIP!
EASY PEASY PENGUIN SQUEEZY.
HAH! I'D LIKE TO SEE A MALLARD TRY SUCH A **DEATH DEFYING** -
DUCK, SIR.
NO, SKIPPER -
DUCK!

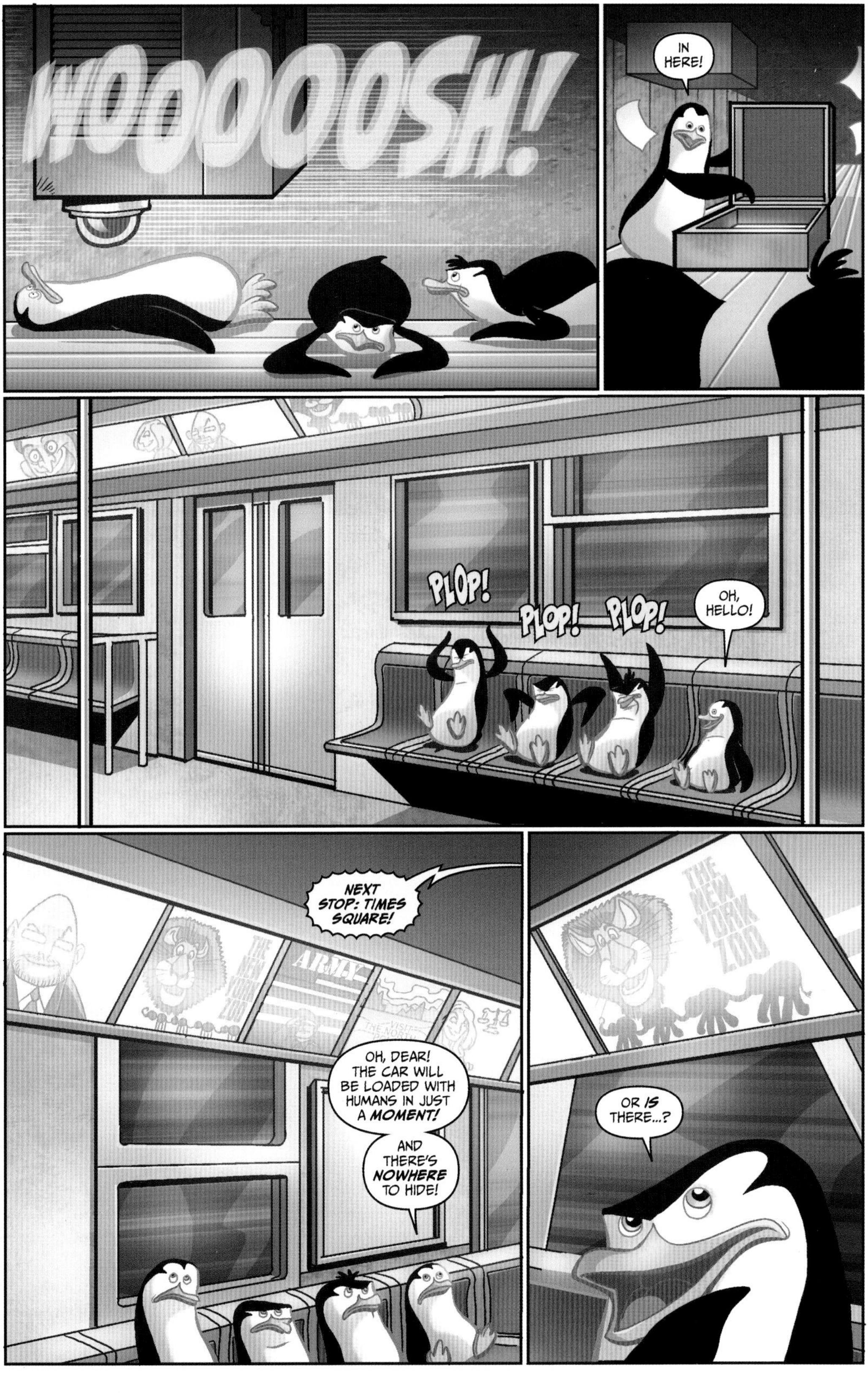
WOOOOOOSH!
IN HERE!
PLOP!
PLOP!
PLOP!
OH, HELLO!
NEXT STOP: TIMES SQUARE!
ARMY
THE NEW YORK ZOO
OH, DEAR! THE CAR WILL BE LOADED WITH HUMANS IN JUST A *MOMENT!*
AND THERE'S *NOWHERE* TO HIDE!
THE NEW YORK ZOO
OR *IS* THERE...?

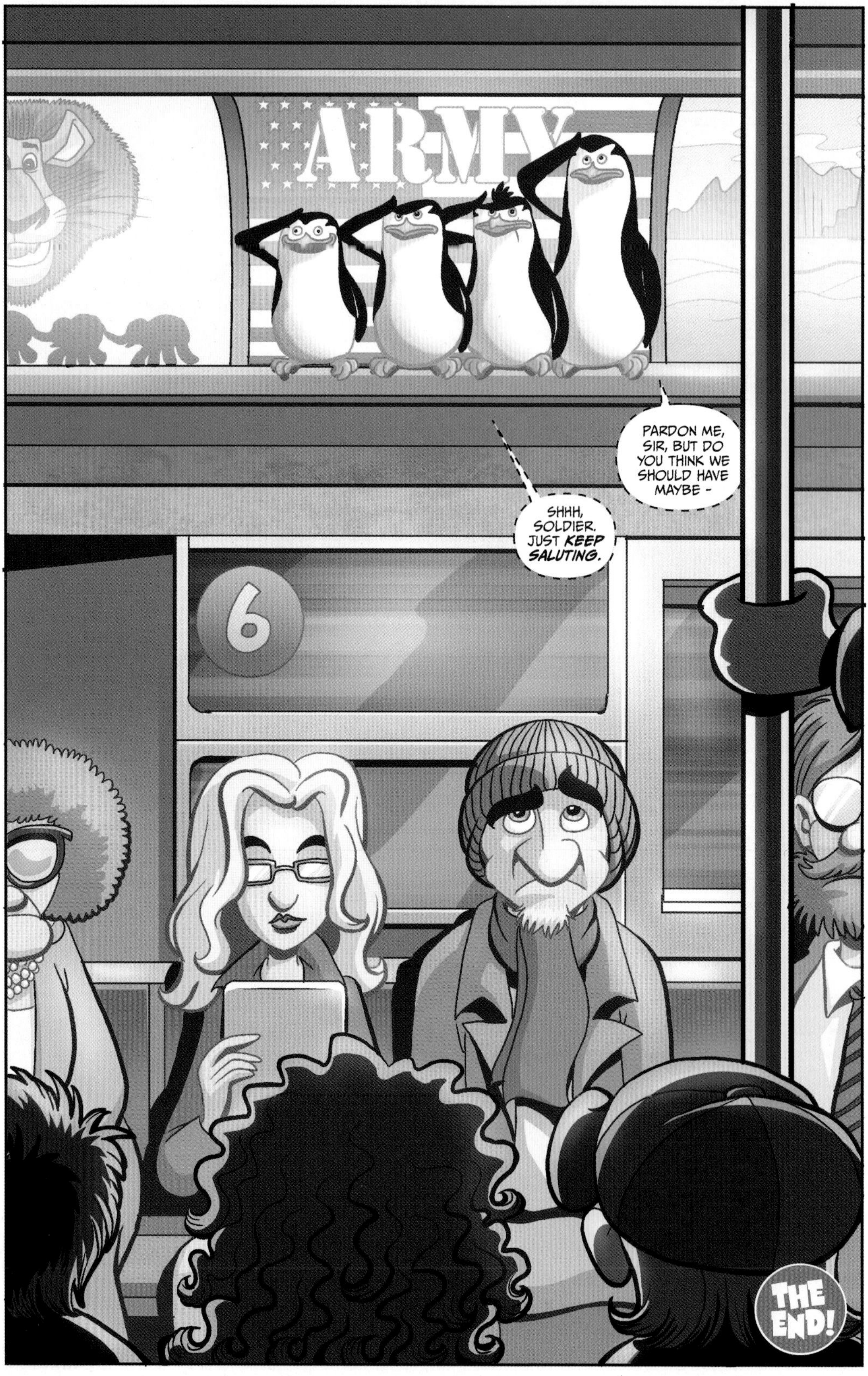
ARMY
PARDON ME, SIR, BUT DO YOU THINK WE SHOULD HAVE MAYBE -
SHHH, SOLDIER. JUST KEEP SALUTING.
6
THE END!

KOWALSKI

THE UNIT'S RESIDENT SCIENCE SUPER WHIZ, KOWALSKI NEVER MET A PROBLEM HE DIDN'T ACCELERATE TO DANGEROUSLY UNSTABLE MOLECULAR PROPORTIONS. A WELL MEANING MAD GENIUS WITH A PENCHANT FOR GIZMOS AND AN ADVANCED DEGREE IN GADGETRY, THIS BRAINY BIRD PUTS THE 'BEAK' BACK IN 'BEAKER'. AND THEN HE MELTS IT. WITH LASERS.

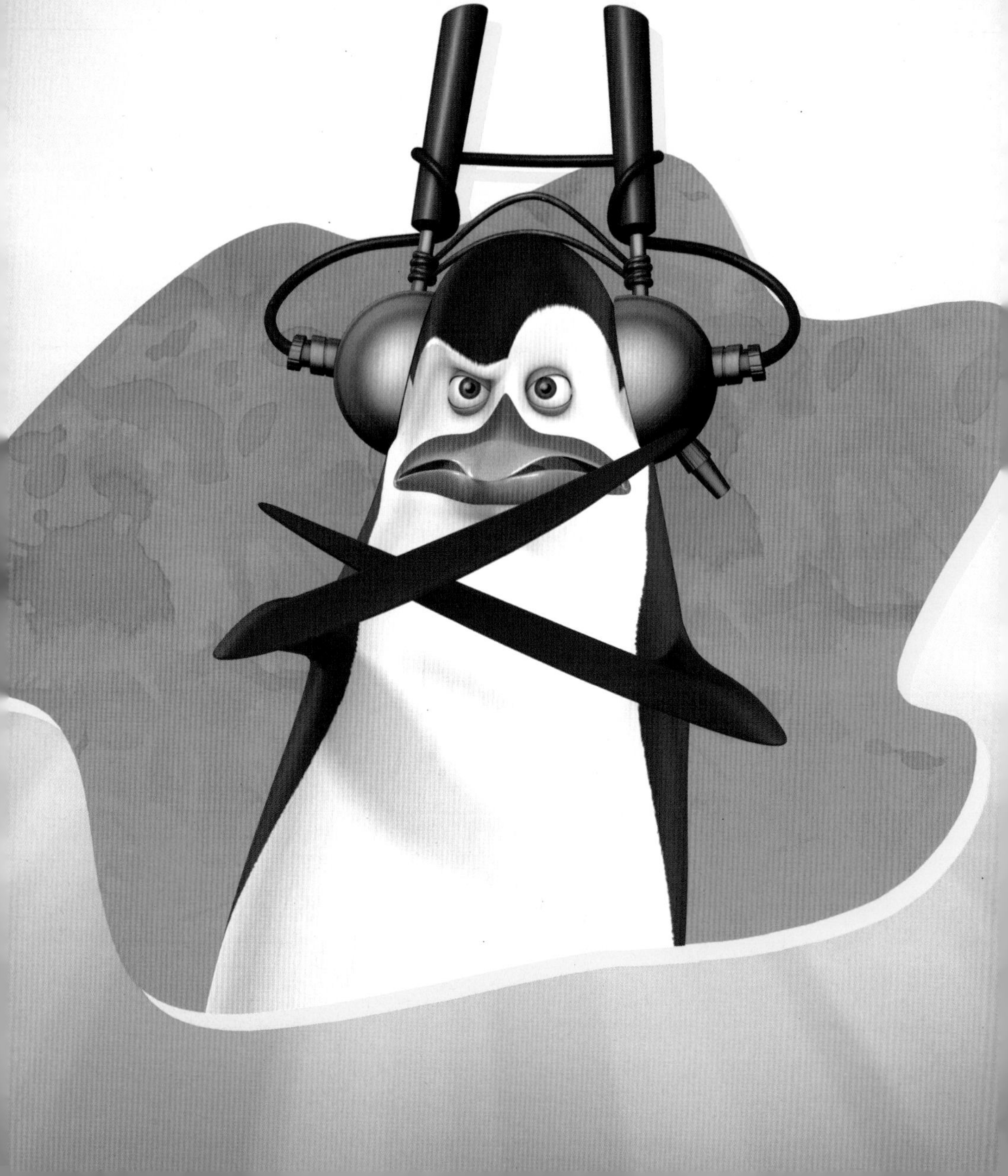

THE SILENT-BUT-DEADLY DEMOLITIONS EXPERT, RICO IS AN UNPREDICTABLE WILDCARD IN THE PENGUIN OPERATION. WITH A SEEMINGLY INEXHAUSTIBLE ARSENAL OF TOOLS AND WEAPONS KEPT SAFELY IN HIS STOMACH, RICO IS ALWAYS READY TO "HORK" UP JUST THE RIGHT ITEM TO SAVE THE DAY. JUST DON'T ASK HIM HOW HE GOT THAT SCAR...

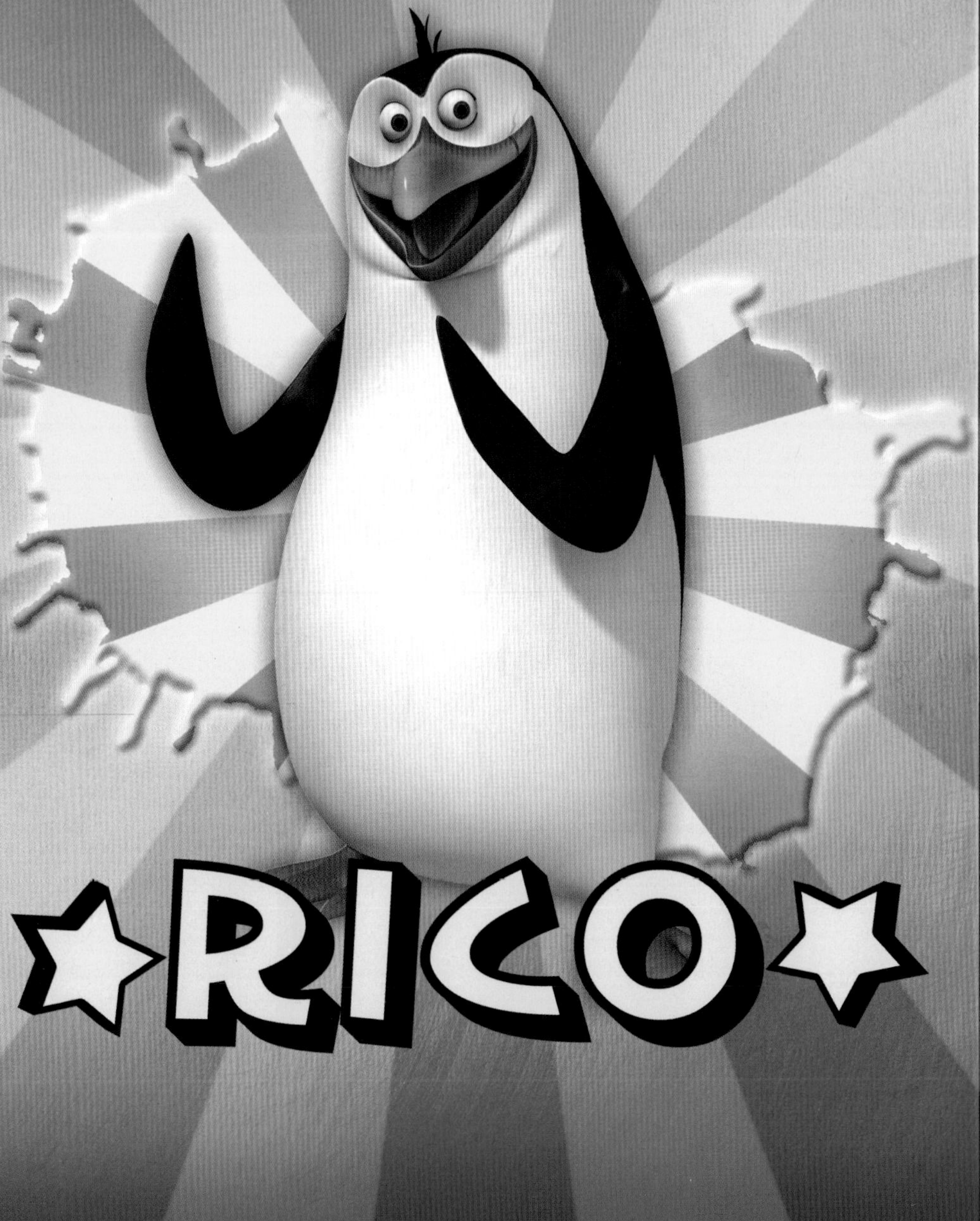
RICO

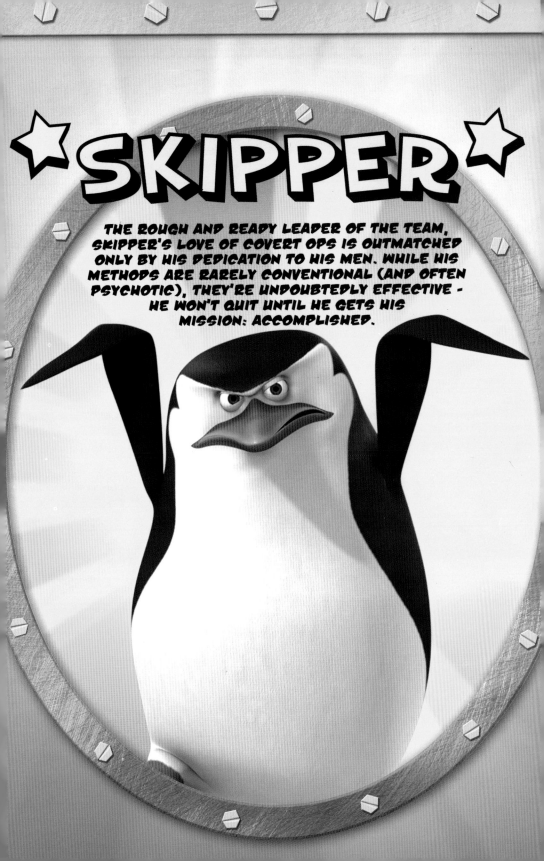

★ SKIPPER ★

THE ROUGH AND READY LEADER OF THE TEAM, SKIPPER'S LOVE OF COVERT OPS IS OUTMATCHED ONLY BY HIS DEDICATION TO HIS MEN. WHILE HIS METHODS ARE RARELY CONVENTIONAL (AND OFTEN PSYCHOTIC), THEY'RE UNDOUBTEDLY EFFECTIVE - HE WON'T QUIT UNTIL HE GETS HIS MISSION: ACCOMPLISHED.

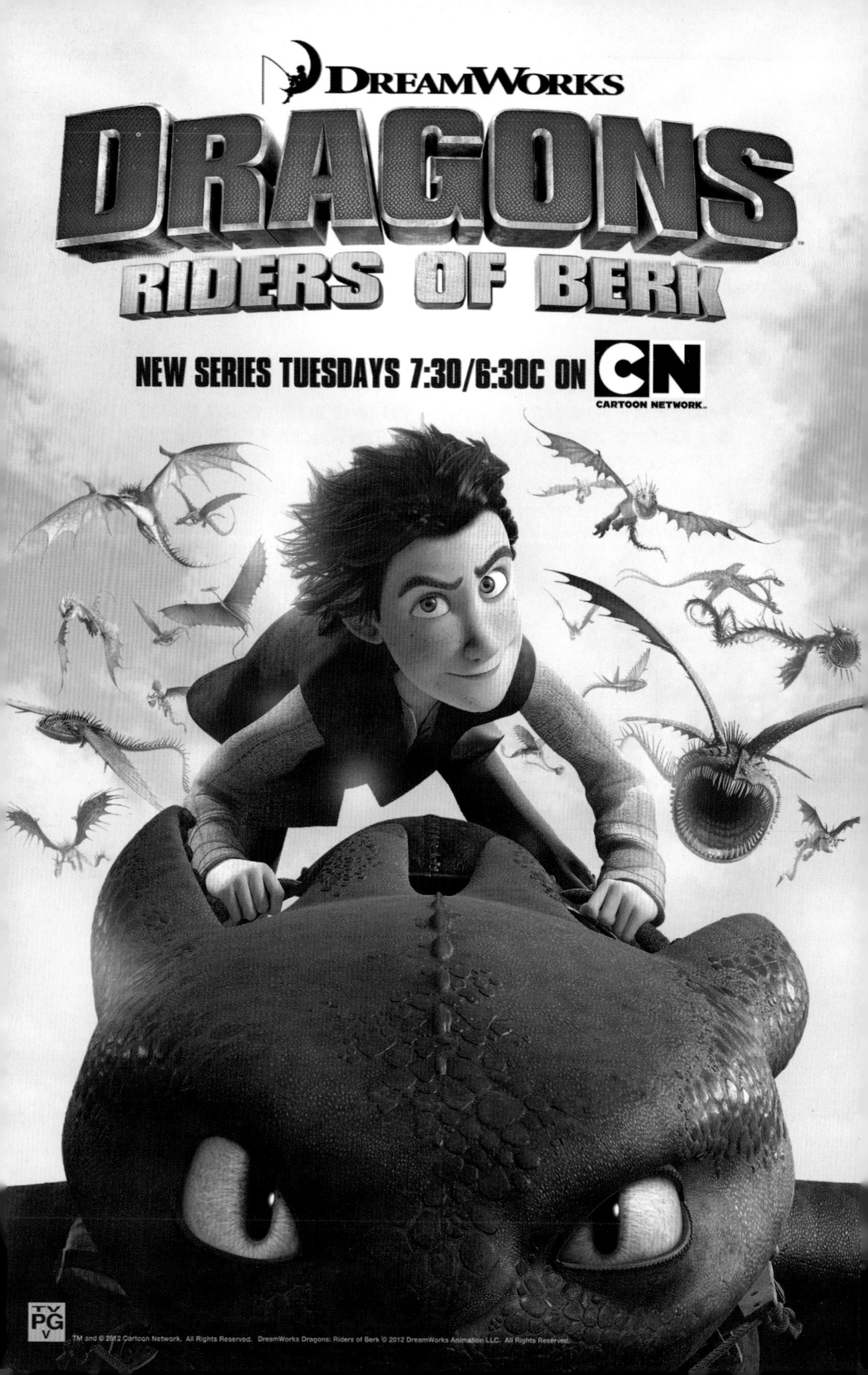
DreamWorks
DRAGONS
RIDERS OF BERK
NEW SERIES TUESDAYS 7:30/6:30C ON CN
CARTOON NETWORK.
TV PG V
TM and © 2012 Cartoon Network. All Rights Reserved. DreamWorks Dragons: Riders of Berk © 2012 DreamWorks Animation LLC. All Rights Reserved.